The Operational Risk Handbook for Financial Companies

A guide to the new world of performance-oriented operational risk

by Brian Barnier

HARRIMAN HOUSE LTD

3A Penns Road
Petersfield
Hampshire
GU32 2EW
GREAT BRITAIN

Tel: +44 (0)1730 233870
Fax: +44 (0)1730 233880
Email: enquiries@harriman-house.com
Website: www.harriman-house.com

First published in Great Britain in 2011 by Harriman House.

978-0857190536

British Library Cataloguing in Publication Data
A CIP catalogue record for this book can be obtained from the British Library.

Printed in the UK by Lightning Source.

Contents

About the Author

US-based Brian Barnier uses his practical cross-discipline, cross-country and cross-industry experience to help leaders improve their personal and operational risk program efficiency and effectiveness. In addition, he has been honored to serve on several industry and professional practice committees, contributing risk management approaches to improve business performance and demonstrate compliance. He was named one of the exclusive fellows of the OCEG (Open Compliance and Ethics Group).

Mr Barnier is a contributor to *Risk Management in Finance* (2009) by Wiley & Sons. He has served as a co-author of ISACA's Risk IT based on COBIT Framework and Practitioner's Guide; as a member of the review committee for OCEG's *Redbook 2.0*, guidance for using governance, risk and compliance to improve principled business performance; and as a member of several committees of the BITS/Financial Services Roundtable.

He teaches professional education in risk management and audit of risk management; has taught operations and finance at the graduate level; has presented popular webinars and podcasts; is regularly quoted in the press; and has over 100 published articles for business operations, finance, technology, audit, risk, security and business continuity audiences. He serves on the editorial panels of the Taylor & Francis EDP Audit, Control and Security (EDPACS) Newsletter, ISACA Journal and the Association for Financial Professionals Risk! newsletter.

www.brianbarnier.com
www.valuebridgeadvisors.com
www.twitter.com/brian_barnier

Acknowledgements

It was a chilly day in New England when an email arrived from Chris Parker of Harriman House—"Ever given any thought to writing a book for professionals?" That simple question not only kicked off this book, but also forced me to more systematically understand and respond to the challenges and needs of operational risk management professionals than ever before. As Chris and I talked further, the thought emerged of a book in which to collect the tools of operational risk management (ORM) as part of a new approach that emphasized performance rather than mere compliance. This too was a 'light bulb' moment. Typical tools have been a loose assortment, without the framework context found in other risk disciplines. Further, many tools were missing from the toolbox.

For help in the initial formation of the book, much appreciation goes to my friend and collaborator on other projects, Gabriel David. His long history in operational risk translated into comments that improved focus, structure and content selections. The book was designed to be more than just a summary or update of what practitioners were doing. Thus, selecting the points of emphasis was crucial. For this, I also owe thanks to operational risk friends who shared their successes and struggles, commented on past articles and asked the tough questions that led to the topics selected.

As I listened to those questions, challenges and needs, many practitioners expressed a desire to know 'what the board wants' or wished their board members would 'get ops risk'. This led to creating the panel of board members, with perspectives from institutions of different sizes. This panel was outstanding in providing time for conversations and reviews. Many thanks go to Marshall Carter, W. Ronald Dietz, Mark Olsen, Karen Osar, Humphrey Polanen and Richard Sergel for sharing their valuable insight and perspective to anchor the book in their rich experience—both as current board members and in their diverse range of past roles. A very special thank you goes to Marshall Carter for sharing his wealth of sometimes very personal experience that set the tone through the Foreword and provided the 'plan B' emphasis throughout the book.

In addition to the board members, another group provided critical content. The systems approach to risk is a touchstone in the book. Bringing their deep experience from diverse areas to bear were Christopher Hart, James Bagian, Jeffrey Pellegrino and John Bresland. Each is a widely recognized leader in his discipline. Deborah Cernauskas, Gabriel David and Tony Tarantino contributed the chapter on capital estimates to help readers avoid common pitfalls. Thank you all for your time and wisdom.

Some content started long before Chris's email arrived—long, long ago in a place far away. For inspiring the chapter on product management and fraud, thanks go to Merle Crawford, an outstanding professor of product management at the University of Michigan who instilled in me a lifelong appreciation of the discipline and became a role model in teaching style. Thanks also to Greg Ulferts, former dean at the University of Detroit Mercy, for the opportunity early in my career to teach both operations management and financial management and thus see risk from both perspectives—the start of my interdisciplinary approach to risk management.

More recently, thanks go to many friends at ISACA, OCEG, RMA, The IIA, BITS/FS Roundtable and other organizations for their insights and experience over the years. It's been an honor serving on committees and teaching with you. Among these good people, special thanks go to my frequent teaching colleague, Urs Fischer. He's both given me insight and helped improve clarity. Of course, thanks to all who have attended the professional education programs I've taught. Your questions have forced me to rethink and refine to meet your needs. Appreciation also goes to those in the regulatory community who helped me better understand regulatory intent and provided comments.

As the draft became more solid, another writing partner became a key reviewer. George Westerman's critique of the framework, flow and content selections was penetrating as he guided me to sharpen. I only hope I was able to fully do justice to all his comments.

Throughout the project, many thanks go to Chris Parker, who became my editor, for pushing me to refine flow and content to improve clarity. Thanks are also due to Louise Hinchen and others at Harriman House for all their work to bring the project to fruition. Appreciation also to Dan Swanson for his encouragement throughout the project. For assistance in assembling the panel of board members, thanks go to my colleagues Chuck Gibson, Nancy May and Priya Cherian Huskins—it is really a surprisingly small world.

In addition to all those above for their comments, thanks also to reviewers Masatoshi Kajimoto, Marcelo Héctor González and Norman Marks. Your critiques and refinements were all appreciated, especially the comments to help make the book more accessible to readers around the globe.

To all these thought-provoking and generous people, my sincere thanks for all that is valuable to the reader.

Finally, and most importantly, much appreciation goes to my wife Carol, for her encouragement and inspiration. If the book reads a bit livelier, the credit goes to her. And, to her and our children Glenn, Katie and Emma for tolerating my time away from them. I look forward to much more time with you all. Love you dearly.

Preface

It's business: Changing economic, competitive, natural and regulatory environments are forcing more emphasis on managing risk in business operations as institutions acquire, divest, launch new products, enter new geographic areas, consolidate and/or seek efficiency gains.

It's business and it's personal: 'I want to keep the boss/board/regulators happy' or 'I need more resources to meet objectives'.

It's just plain personal: 'I want to finish working before midnight!'

Operational risk is important to financial companies for three key reasons:

1. **Bottom-line impact**. Without operations, there is no business—and without managing operational risk there will soon be no operations. Operations are the range of activities that create, sell and deliver products and services to customers. This includes product management, accounting, processing, IT, call centers, and branch operations. Weaknesses in operations are simply bad for business. Operational weaknesses slow product improvement, hurt customer service, and slow expansion and acquisition. Errors, waste, theft, fraud and penalties all add needless cost. Capital held aside for operational risk reduces earning power. Collectively, this hurts global and local economic performance.

2. **Operational activities drive financial results**. Effective operational risk is therefore key not only to minimizing loss but to maximizing profit. It influences, for instance, product launch-cycle time, product accessibility, market share, market growth rate, transaction-processing times, costs per transaction, IT cost and responsiveness, IT service quality and customer satisfaction.

3. **Regulatory and contractual compliance is required**. Growing legal obligations in all territories mean that operational risk is simply no longer optional (if indeed it ever was).

Who this book is for

This book is primarily for operational risk leaders who seek practical insights to improve the maturity of their operational risk function. It accomplishes this by introducing them to a range of innovative and proven new approaches.

It's for leaders who:

- are wondering: 'Is there more to operational risk than compliance paperwork?'

- realize there must be a better way to deliver for their boards and regulators, and that doing more of the same won't work

- are outgrowing their current toolkit and realize they need more efficient and effective tools/methods/techniques if they are going to produce better business results

- are already curious about what works in other disciplines in their institution that must manage risk—such as strategy, business continuity, process improvement or quality control (QC)—and wonder what that implies for operational risk

- are wondering, 'What works?' in other industries as they manage risk to operations

- want to make a personal difference in managing risk to business return.

Other roles can also benefit:

- board members—seeking insight to guide and oversee their operational risk function

- auditors—needing to discharge their responsibility to audit risk management (they can convert the suggested management actions into audit inquiries)

- business leaders—who want to understand how to engage the operational risk function to help reduce risk to operational performance and optimize use of capital in operations.

What this book does

This book is about the business. It takes the perspective of managing risk to the business in a dynamic institution. This is in contrast to managing an operational risk function. The latter too often says: 'We're managing a function and we need to embed in the organization.' Instead, this book says, 'We're running a business and need risk management (like financial or human resource management) to enable our success.' It's a subtle but powerful shift in perspective—to an institution and personally to a risk leader.

This book is practical. It's not about theory or complex mathematical models for capital estimates. Rather, the focus is twofold. First, it is on enabling the shift from a compliance- to a *performance*-based approach to risk management, to help institutions realize that it is in their own self-interest to have a solid operational risk management approach. Second, the focus is on the important preparatory steps to capital estimates—understanding how an enterprise works in its environment. The central tool it introduces is life-like scenario analysis for understanding risk in a *system*: how chains of events cascade from root-cause problems to consequences. Bad things don't happen by magic. They result from causes. This understanding is fundamental for better risk management and for more reliable capital estimates.

This book is practical because it grew out of three particular sources. First, it evolved out of my public and private presentations to and feedback from over 4000 professionals working in or with risk management in the past two years. This includes professionals at industry events and in their individual enterprises. Whether presenting from a managerial or audit perspective, these were two-way conversations to understand problems, seek out root causes and build on the advances we made together. Second, it grew out of research with business and IT leaders. It's amazing how little is really known about what is efficient and effective in risk management. As described in chapter 2.6, a colleague at the Massachusetts Institute of Technology (MIT) and I surveyed executives in seven countries on both effectiveness and organizational perceptions of effectiveness. It was a first. Third, this book also embraces the experiences of those with whom I serve on standards, practices and guidance committees. Together, this tapestry of perspectives creates a body of knowledge on operational risk that till now has not been collected in one volume. For you, the reader, it brings this breadth of insight to you in your role in financial services.

This book is not a repeat of commonly discussed topics. Nor is it a thorough academic text. Common tools such as risk control self-assessments, loss-data collection, key risk indicators, scenario analysis or capital estimates are mentioned, but it is in the context of using them in a more mature, performance-focused approach. The focus is on those areas that raise the most questions and provide immediate opportunities for improvement.

The right tool for the right job

A continual and overriding interest in *how* to implement better operational risk management has driven this book's emphasis on tools: actionable techniques and methods for superior performance.

Tools make your job easier and/or more efficient. In our personal lives, we've all worked on some hobby or project: cooking, gardening, hunting, skiing, fishing, boating, stained glass, or violin. The better we get, the more we need better tools. In the same way, the basic tools of Basel-era operational risk are no longer sufficient for our challenges. As we will see, we can use proven tools from other areas of our institutions, disciplines and industries to help us mature more quickly and easily. Teaming with other disciplines engages knowledge and saves resources—it's efficient and effective.

The book is organized to present practical tools you can use in a better-integrated process of managing risk. The tools and this process have been carefully adapted to the operational risk needs of financial companies from related processes used in other disciplines and industries with similar needs. The hope is that this approach makes it easier to create, use and continually improve a risk management process, makes tools more accessible, and makes it easier to learn from others who have applied these tools.

If you're ready to shift to a more performance-focused and systematic approach to operational risk management, I hope that this guidance will make it easier for you to get there and personally bring more value to your institution.

Brian Barnier
Connecticut, 2011

Foreword—Marshall Carter on Plan B Thinking

Risk is real. Real processes must work, and real dependencies must be faced because real environments shift constantly and the real laws of physics never change. To respond to risk, a back-up plan is needed. In the event that the initial plan (plan A) is no longer possible, we need a *plan B*. That back-up plan is driven by the reality of risk, options to contain it, options to stop it and options to shift with it.

Starting his career as a Marine infantry officer in Vietnam and carrying through to his current passion as a private pilot, Marshall Carter doesn't have the luxury of seeing risk management as simply a compliance exercise. He has a career punctuated by thriving in risky situations. In his current role as chairman of the (New York Stock Exchange) NYSE group and deputy chairman of NYSE Euronext, he was brought in to oversee the repair and transformation of that venerable stock exchange, which included the acquisition of Archipelago, conversion to a publicly traded company and merger with Euronext. Prior to this, he was chairman and CEO of State Street Corporation, which he grew sixfold. In earlier roles at Chase Manhattan Bank, he spent 15 years fixing problems and improving performance.

Academically, he was well prepared to do this, with a degree in engineering from the US Military Academy at West Point, a master's degree in operations research and systems analysis from the US Naval Postgraduate School, and a second master's degree in science, technology and public policy from The George Washington University.

In Vietnam, Marsh Carter was awarded the Purple Heart and the Navy Cross (the next highest award to the Congressional Medal of Honor). He received the Navy Cross for heroism in crawling toward enemy lines to rescue a fallen soldier and then single-handedly throwing grenades toward the enemy to provide cover for his troops to safely evacuate. From the bomb-churned fields of Vietnam, Marsh Carter now finds himself on the manicured campuses of the Naval War College and MIT's Sloan School of Management. He spends his time at these institutions sharing lessons learned on battlefields and in boardrooms with rising military and business leaders.

The need for plan B thinking is a painfully learned lesson I've carried all my life. An infantry company runs on its junior leaders—lieutenants, sergeants and corporals. In 1966, on my first tour of duty in Vietnam, on one mission we went into combat with 175 troops. Within six hours, we had 36 killed or wounded, including two of the three lieutenants and six of the nine sergeants.

That experience and many others taught me the need to always, *always* have a plan B that is ready to go.

Thirty years later, I was chairman and CEO of State Street, transforming the over-200-year-old institution from a bank into a technology-based, product-management-focused company providing custodial and asset-management services. We were taking risks in acquisitions, new technology investments and new products. The quality and readiness of our plan B was a measure of our risk management because it embodied all we knew about both the range and nature of the risks that faced us and our range of potential responses. For example, once I received a phone call at 2 am. We had a process outage in Australia that had shut down our clearing and settlement services for a number of our Asia-Pacific customers. The problem? A squirrel chewing on wires. But we had—and implemented—a plan B that responded to that specific kind of risk to operations. Likewise, we had a plan B for risks that extended all the way to the top, with a well-defined succession plan for the role of CEO.

Ten years on from this, on December 1 2007, I was chairman of the NYSE group and deputy chairman of NYSE Euronext. Our CEO, John Thain, had just been hired away by Merrill Lynch. Yet we were prepared. We knew this was a risk for an executive of John's calibre and had started a silent search over a year earlier. We had assembled a list of 30 potential successors. At the top of that list was Duncan Niederauer. We hired Duncan as our president and co-COO in April of 2007. When John was selected as CEO of Merrill Lynch about six months later, it took the transatlantic board about an hour to announce Duncan as successor—with whom we had been pleased since he came aboard.

The rising challenge of operational risk for financial services

The complexity of real systems and operations is one of two reasons why operational risk is so challenging. The other is because financial institutions are constantly taking on more and more operational risk as they change their business models. Traditional risks (credit) are shrinking as a proportion of total risk. This change is striking in institutions such as State Street and NYSE that are becoming far more dependent on technology, creating new products and expanding geographically. It is also there in small community banks responding to the needs of small business customers who want integrated access to all accounts and want that access fully integrated with their accounting software.

This change and the growing importance of operations in the performance of an institution means that boards and CEOs are more concerned than ever with risk to operations that can hurt performance. This is why the role of operational risk leader has never been more important. And it's why operational risk leaders need to be smart in using the right approaches and techniques to help business leaders manage that risk.

Three hurdles

As I look across my career managing risk to operational performance, there seem to be three recent hurdles to the success of operational risk managers.

First, there is the amount and pace of change in the financial services business. It is difficult to understand the business products and processes (and gaps) well enough to help business leaders reduce risk to performance. At Chase Manhattan in the 1980s, we had detailed pre-launch product reviews with a dozen people on a team to look for risk root causes and address them. Today, the challenge is to maintain such discipline across more and new types of products.

Second, there is the increased complexity of systems and technology. Stock exchanges, banks and other financial institutions have been humbled by technology failures. Others have lagged because they have not been quick enough to adopt. At both State Street and the NYSE, I was on a sprint to make smart acquisitions of technology and technology-based service companies that would help us to grow profitable revenue with less risk. Many companies struggle to adopt and integrate this technology, wasting huge amounts of money in the process. So operational risk leaders have the challenge of digging down through the product process and technology layers to understand dependencies and root causes.

Third, there is the confusion between compliance and operational risk management that takes focus away from managing risk. Today, I read too often of risk management as a compliance exercise. The need to manage risk to operations existed long before SOX, Basel II and Solvency II. Compliance must be done. Yet, a danger arises if institutions don't sufficiently manage risk because they are mostly doing compliance. As a pilot, I do risk management to arrive safely at my destination, not just because the FAA says so. At State Street and NYSE Euronext, we manage risk to deliver performance to customers and shareholders. Better risk management improves compliance, but compliance alone does not make a high-performing institution risk-free.

Shaping your thinking toward success

These three hurdles to success frame the need for three key kinds of action, all of which are explored at length in this book.

First, know the business, understand it is a system that works to get tasks done and that each process step has a series of dependencies on other people, processes and technology.

For example, at Chase, we acquired a bank with some small town branches. I went to look at operations, to understand the risks and what we needed to improve. I asked questions, including: "How are transaction receipts delivered from the branches to the main office?" The answer—"The local taxi driver collects them." That was a surprise! It's by understanding each process step—and what can go wrong—that we find risks and learn how to fix root causes.

I saw the same when I was chair of the Boston Medical Center: Proper operational procedures are critical in preventing problems. Today, in financial services, we're living with the consequences of the failure to fully understand the entire system and dependencies in the sub-prime mortgage process, the foreclosure process and products such as credit default swaps.

Second, ask 'Why?' until you get to the root cause. Don't stop at the symptoms. Also, don't easily accept 'unknowns'. By systematically understanding the external environment and internal business process and dependencies, shed light on the unknowns.

In our processing problem at State Street, we had to find the squirrel in the wiring. Then we needed to find out how the squirrel got there and how to keep other pests out. Just think, if Admiral Grace Hopper had found a squirrel in her computer before she had found the moth, we might be calling computing problems 'squirrels' today instead of 'bugs'.

At Chase, to avoid the 'unknowns', we stressed the importance of inviting a range of people to product reviews. The risk manager needs to find out who already knows. That's the best way to avoid 'unknowns'.

Third, focus on reducing risk to performance. In approach, this implies closely tying risk management to performance management. This nicely aligns performance and related risk measures—such as the risk of transactions taking longer than a specified objective. Avoid being distracted by compliance or capital model reports, they are only a few of many reports and they don't actually fix risk. For example, acquisitions are intended to drive major performance improvement. They also have significant risks. At State Street, I had specific guidelines for acquisitions to avoid excessive risk. Then we had to carefully manage the risks we did take to achieve the expected performance.

Taking these three thoughts together, you can acquire the insight you need to create life-like scenarios that help you understand the real nature of the risk and your range of options. And then you can create meaningful plan Bs.

Plan B in your pocket

When it comes to devising that plan B, you need to remember that plan Bs come in two flavors.

One is *straightforward*, such as when John Thain was selected as CEO of Merrill Lynch, we had the replacement ready. In the extreme, this type can be automated, such as in trading systems or computer back-up systems. These work best for well-defined situations and/or where large numbers of people must be trained to take an action (such as evacuate a building due to fire or respond to a bank robbery).

The second, and more broadly needed, type stresses *defined decision-making steps to evaluate and respond to a set of circumstances*. Examples of such circumstances might include the exposure of a large fraud, a natural disaster, or a major competitor's announcement. These are better addressed as dynamic threat environments, such as those I experience every time I pilot my seaplane. These require advanced planning and clear thinking so that your plan's scope has room for detecting and responding to a range of unknowns.

So a good plan B of the second type contains information on what triggers to look for, how they might unfold, and how to respond in order to both contain the unfolding chain of events (if possible) and remedy the consequences. Of course, the plan can't contain this information unless the scenario is well thought through in the first place. That requires real risk analysis, well beyond checklist compliance. That's why a big value of any plan B is as a check on the quality of risk understanding. This depth of understanding is needed to get to potential root causes (such as what gaps allow frauds to occur) to actually prevent problems.

A good plan B in your pocket means you understand the environment, the business process, your capabilities, what can go wrong and your options. It means you know what to do when a chain of events starts cascading your way and, whenever possible, how to prevent it. Self-assessments and status reports make pretty pictures on computer screens. Yet, at the end of the day, I want plan B in my pocket—whether on the battlefield or in the boardroom.

For operational risk leaders in our changing and complex environment, mastering the plan B is your opportunity to make a difference in your institution.

Marshall Carter
Massachusetts, 2011

Introduction

Touchstones to Keep Focus on Efficiency and Effectiveness

- We all manage risk; it's part of life.
- Risk management is simple.
- Life and business are complex.
- Use risk management approaches to make business simpler as one way to reduce risk.
- Use risk management to provide clarity and logic, not emotion and bias.
- Use the right tools to make the job easier.

This book describes an approach to help **financial companies shift to a more business *performance*-oriented, systematic approach to risk management**. To this end, it is helpful to be focused by a set of touchstones.

The following will be elaborated and borne out over the coming chapters, but they are collected here in preview for ease of reference and to set out, as it were in blueprint, the practical implications of this book.

Overall

The best risk management is about *managing risk to business performance* against *specific outcomes or objectives*.

- Changing situations may bring gain or loss.

- Risk management is not a paperwork exercise for compliance. Compliance will always leave gaps and exposures to real business risk that can harm customers, partners and shareholders. Look at the litter of companies over the years who have been compliant and still suffered loss.

- Risk management should *improve agility*, making it safer to move in a changing environment.

Risk evaluation

Root cause is the key to finding and fixing risks to performance—especially to finding problems early and fixing them fast.

A *systems* view of risk is needed to understand the *dependencies* of products on processes, people and technology.

- An 'event' is not isolated. Potential and realized risks are *chains* of events that cascade in time, triggered by causes in dependencies or other related events.

- Thus, risks must be analyzed in *robust scenarios* that consider environments, systems and cascades to understand how situations might be prevented and, when they arise, contained.

- Scenarios are therefore the central feature of risk evaluation.

Little is truly new in the world. This is especially true of root causes, although consequences play out differently due to different environments. After each situation arises, people often emerge who have already tried to call attention to the problem.

- A key role of the operational risk manager in conducting scenario analysis workshops is simply to *ensure that the right people are in the room* to bring their insight to the discussion of how products and processes work in systems—the dependencies, the timing, the gaps and what is already broken or likely to break under stress.

- You must *push to see enough* to understand potential problems and opportunities in a changing environment.

Understand the business *value of your options*: the value of knowing now, rather than later; the value of acting now, rather than later—having *more time to act*; and the value of having a range of options, rather than being forced into one.

Risk response

Always have a plan B. Use this not only to prevent and prepare, but also to test the quality of your risk evaluation.

- Base responses on *root-cause data,* which can provide early warnings and point to what to fix, not proximate-cause data.

- View *risk-status data in the context of cascading events in time* created earlier in scenario analysis. This gives meaning to 'What could happen next?' and provides insight for action. This is *situational awareness*. Look for changes and *patterns* that create the need to act.

- Use plan Bs to guide you under pressure to take the *right action*, instead of making the situation worse. Consider the cost/benefit of each of the range of options.

Risk oversight

More *risk-return-aware decisions* form the best path to reducing risk to performance.

Ensure board-level (especially independent member) engagement in operational risk:

- First, make certain that the board risk *committee has skill* in risk management and a wide range of risk types.

- Second, make sure that the chief risk officer has clear authority and 'voice' to the board.

- Lastly, ensure that levels of assurance are matched to the nature of risks. 'Reasonable assurance' used for risk to financial statement preparation (and audit committees) is not sufficient for managing risk to a business initiative or to human safety.

Continually *improve maturity* of risk management *capability*:

- Stress a culture of *'find early, fix fast'*, with a mandate for open communications (full disclosure, no defensiveness). Become *time-sensitive*.

- Deeply build risk awareness and risk response into your organization. Everyone has a role in preventing and responding.

- *Be humble*. Realize limitations. Understand bias. Seek people, training and past lessons to *overcome blind spots*.

Demand an *end-to-end view* of risk by business activity/product/process— cross the silos.

* * *

Keeping these thoughts in mind, let's see how these points have been reflected in the past in managing risk to operations.[1] We'll take a whirlwind trip through history and then get some practical insights from other industries with similar challenges: insights which are then fleshed out and applied to financial services throughout the rest of the book.

'Been There, Done That'—the Voice of Experience

Marsh Carter opened this book with a view of lessons he learned fixing problems at Chase Manhattan Bank and transforming State Street Corp. Some of his instincts in finding and fixing risk root causes trace back to his experience in the US Marine Corps and his operations research degree from the Naval Postgraduate School. For thousands of years, militaries have been concerned about the science of logistics—"the study of moving and quartering troops".[2]

In this same spirit, it is helpful for us to learn from those who have 'been there, done that' over the years in managing risk to operations. As several notables have observed: "Those who don't know history are destined to repeat it."[3]

In the ancient world

Looking back on the lessons of history, we see that success or failure in operations has led to the rise and fall of civilizations. Alexander the Great (356–323 BC) faced this in the expansion of his empire. This enlargement required him to quickly create government operations that communicated

---

[1] Because risk terminology varies among professional disciplines, please note that in this book, 'risk to operations' refers to risks to an institution's ability to conduct business—creating, marketing, selling, delivering and servicing some offering that generates profitable revenue. Following Basel, this excludes 'pure' financial risks (credit and market) and strategic risks. That said, operations are deeply intertwined with credit and market considerations. With respect to strategic risks, this embraces the operational aspects, such as ability to integrate an acquisition or execute on a geographic or product expansion. 'Operational risk' is used as defined in the Basel accords and Solvency II. 'Operations risk' is sometimes used to refer to risk in back-office operations or transaction systems; it is not used separately in this book. For readers in insurers in countries where 'business risk' is used, 'business risk' generally encompasses operational risk.

[2] *OED*.

[3] Edmund Burke (1729–1797) has been credited with this phrase. Spanish philosopher George Santayana (1863–1952) wrote: "Those who cannot remember the past are condemned to repeat it" in *The Life of Reason*. Sir Winston Churchill (1874–1965) echoed the thought by saying: "Those that fail to learn from history, are doomed to repeat it."

from Greece in the northwest to Egypt in the southwest, as well as to what is now western India in the East. Hannibal, the military leader from Carthage (248–183/2 BC), also managed severe and extensive risk to operations when he successfully crossed the Alps with war elephants into northern Italy in 218 BC. The Romans recognized the need for effective operations to hold their empire together by building good roads and a postal system. Almost 2000 years later, Napoleon's failure to learn about risk to operations contributed to his disastrous march on Moscow during 1812 and 1813.

Rulers in the ancient world also had to evaluate the likelihood of success or failure as they shifted their alliances and tribute. After Alexander the Great's death and the division of his kingdom among his four leading generals, a period of shifts and conflicts ensued until the Romans gained control (with operations management success playing a non-trivial role on both the military and civilian construction fronts). The success or failure of operations is seen even in Biblical history. In the Book of Luke, a civil engineering failure is reported. Eighteen people were killed when the Tower of Siloam collapsed.[4] In the Book of Acts, it is reported that St Paul is forced to winter on Malta after his shipwreck. We learn why from Roman maritime law. Navigation was allowed (*secura navigatio*) from March 10 through October. Then, after an interim period, navigation was closed (*mare clausum*)[5] from late November through February.

Two lessons to learn from these early considerations in logistics and operations are that:

1. The approach addressed both finding and fixing problems more quickly than adversaries (owing to serious competitive time pressure, and not just for market share).

2. It was all 'qualitative' by our standards today.

According to several histories, probability theory didn't arise formally until the mid-1600s with the work of Blaise Pascal and Pierre de Fermat, which focused largely on probabilities in games, such as dice. Christian Huygens wrote a key formalized work in 1657. The first insurance arrangement at Edward Lloyd's coffeehouse began in about 1688. Pierre de Laplace penned a broader view of the subject entitled *Théorie Analytique des Probabilités* in 1812. Too bad Napoleon was busy marching to Moscow; maybe he should have been reading de Laplace's book. This is a powerful learning point for us today in managing risk to operations. Amidst the checklist culture, there is a

---

[4] Luke Chapter 13, Verse 4.

[5] *Oxford Classical Dictionary.*

risk of losing sight of our essential objectives; businesses do not exist simply to exist or get by, but to excel and outperform. Could the risk management processes in our institutions get Alexander to India, Hannibal over the mountains, or build and operate the Roman road and postal systems? Honestly answering this question can be sobering. The good news is that there is much in history from which to learn.

In the past century

Looking back over the past century, we see several advances in operations research and risk management that continue to shape financial companies' approach to operational risk. These include the development of:

- the control chart by Walter A. Shewhart (1891–1967) at Bell Labs in the 1920s

- the option discussion in the *Theory of Interest* by Irving Fisher (1867–1947) in 1930

- the Plan-Do-Check-Act cycle also developed by Shewhart and later termed the Plan-Do-Study-Act cycle by W. Edwards Deming (1900–1993)

- a wide range of statistical risk reduction and quality- and performance-improvement methods driven by Deming in post-WWII Japan, for which he received many honors

- root-cause analysis and quality improvement by Kaoru Ishikawa (1915–1989) at Toyota

- quality improvement by Philip Crosby (1926–2001)

- project management techniques such as the program evaluation review technique developed by Booz Allen Hamilton and the US Navy in 1957 for the Polaris nuclear submarine project, and the critical path method formalized in the late 1950s (based on earlier work by DuPont for the Manhattan Project)

- the option pricing model devised in 1973 by Fischer Black and Myron Scholes that lit the world of derivatives on fire.

This is just a short list focused on operations. Common tools for managing credit or market risk are not included because managing risk to operations is fundamentally different from managing credit or market risk. It would therefore be inappropriate to inherit risk management concepts and tools from credit or market risk, even though superficially we might think they make the most sense for financial companies. Instead, **the best place to get tools that help us improve operational risk management in financial services is in the history of innovations in operational management**.

A recurring focus throughout such tools for managing risk to operations, as we shall see, is the idea of a *system*. **A system generally has inputs/resources, process, outputs, and objectives (including in quantity, quality and time/schedule). It also has specific boundaries and relationships to other systems**. This is basic to processing deposits, checks, loans or insurance claims. Systems also have vulnerabilities or exposures based on the quality of their capabilities. As we will see, **understanding how a system operates is basic to finding and fixing risks to operations**.

The 'new' techniques we'll be looking at are the analytical basis of operational management courses taught by academic and professional association educators to aspiring operations managers. Many professional disciplines rely on these, including product managers, project managers, business continuity managers, crisis managers, IT operations mangers, security managers, facilities managers, purchasing managers and many others.

In this perspective, operational risk is about managing risk to operational performance. Leaders in many industries face similar challenges processing transactions, delivering products, operating branch locations, suffering frauds, in dependencies on IT, keeping data private and/or maintaining continuity in operations. In financial institutions, this includes customer–facing, back–office, IT, vendor management, contract oversight that might be a source of risk to operational or financial performance or have other consequences, such as damage to reputation. [6]

Lessons for risk oversight

Operational risk management in non-financial industries is a rich mine of insight for financial services today because those other industries have always had a natural tendency to focus on risks to operations. Operations are particularly significant sources of risk (downside and upside) for them. Karen Osar, a board member of a bank and a specialty chemicals manufacturing company, explains: "Risk management is high on the agenda of a non-bank

---

[6] For more detail on regulatory definitions, please see chapter 1.8 on capital estimates. In brief, Basel sees 'operational risks' as most risks other than strategic, market and credit.

board on which I serve: The nominating and governance committee oversees risk management. This is to ensure we have the right focus on risks to short- and long-term performance as well as strong oversight of compliance and ethical matters."

Another aspect is oversight of systemic risks. In financial services, significant concern has been expressed about the interconnectedness within the financial system and the ability of problems to spread from one institution to another. This could be the result of cascading failures, such as when a trading or settlement partner has a failure, or gaps in visibility in end-to-end business processes, such as the inability to see across the sub-prime mortgage-lending process from origination through to securitization in secondary markets. Two other industries with significant systemic aspects of operational risk are electric utilities and air transportation. The following case studies show the kind of breakthroughs they have been able to make in tackling systemic risk.

Case study: facing down system risk

In the electric industry, utilities use strict, standards-based top-level governance. Richard Sergel, former CEO of the North American Electric Reliability Corporation (NERC), explains; "In North America, the industry is self-regulated within a framework approved by the various government jurisdictions. The utilities vote for themselves on standards and then our job in NERC is to vigorously enforce them. To have a system, we must know what everyone is going to do. We have real-time visibility of the system and conduct post-incident reviews of problems."

In air transportation, there are multiple levels of oversight. National legislation and regulatory agencies provide legal oversight. However, there are also non-regulatory agencies and partnerships to manage risk and improve safety. In the United States, the National Transportation Safety Board (NTSB) is an independent, non-regulatory agency charged with determining the probable cause of transportation accidents, promoting transportation safety, and assisting victims of transportation accidents and their families.

To help prevent accidents, the NTSB develops safety recommendations based on investigations and studies. The Honorable Christopher A. Hart is the vice-chairman of the NTSB, an attorney and aerospace engineer. He is impassioned in stressing the importance of a systems view of risk: "The catalyst that energized the airline community to develop ways to further improve safety was the realization in the mid-1990s that their fatal accident rate, which had been declining for many years, was no longer declining but was stuck on a plateau. The concern was that, given the anticipated increase in airline volume—it was widely predicted to double in the next 15 years or so—a flat accident rate multiplied by an increasing volume of activity would result in an unacceptable number of accidents. Hence, **the US airline industry created a goal of reducing the fatal accident rate by 80% in ten years**. The process that was used to pursue this goal may be unique to the aviation industry—both before and since. The industry created the Commercial Aviation Safety Team (CAST), in which all segments of the industry—airlines, manufacturers, pilots, air traffic control, and the regulator—came to the table to work collaboratively to (1) identify safety concerns, (2) prioritize those concerns, (3) develop remedies for the prioritized concerns, and (4) evaluate the effectiveness of the remedies.

"The fuel for the CAST process started with information about daily operations from aircraft flight data recorders and pilot reporting programs. In order for front-line workers to participate in and agree to the collection of information about daily front-line operations, management and the regulator had to assure those workers that the information would not (unless the information revealed criminal or intentional wrongdoing) be used against them in any way. Although the US airline safety record was already considered exemplary in the mid-1990s, this process was so successful that it resulted in a 65% reduction in the fatal accident rate in only ten years—from 1997 to 2007."

Founded in 1998, CAST developed an integrated, data-driven strategy to reduce the commercial aviation fatality risk in the United States and promote new government and industry safety initiatives throughout the world. In 2009, CAST was awarded the prestigious Collier Trophy for their success in improving safety through a systems analysis approach that engaged a wide variety of the industry.

This approach to systems is especially important today in our complex environment where problems result from multiple causes. For example, when US Air Flight 1549 made an emergency landing on the Hudson River in January 2009, there were bird strikes in both engines that were severe enough to cause engine failures. Also over the Hudson River eight months later was the crash of a sightseeing helicopter and a small fixed-wing aircraft that killed nine people. In that situation, there was a combination of air traffic controller inattention, lack of clarity in radio frequency change, weakness in the design of the traffic separation zones and unfortunate alignment of aircraft such that it was difficult for the fixed-wing pilot to see a helicopter in front of buildings. Repeatedly, it's been demonstrated that it is critical to have a deep understanding of the entire system and have oversight that engages the right parties with the right information to make better decisions to reduce risk for the traveling public. [7]

---

[7] NTSB investigation reports on these and other accidents are at: **www.ntsb.gov/Publictn/publictn.htm**

Lessons from risk evaluation

In evaluating risks, three lessons seem to be highly applicable to current questions in financial services.

Scenario analysis

First, in scenario analysis. Other industries have taught us that scenarios need to be more realistic in addressing real threats to real operations—and the performance of those operating processes—than what banks have used for long-tail testing. Various industries and disciplines provide guidance on scenario analysis. For example, airlines must look at complex scenarios resulting from weather disruptions to service. Manufacturers, distributors, and retailers must evaluate scenarios ranging from a shortage of parts to labor actions. In financial institutions today, guidance on scenario analysis for CFOs and business continuity planners can be adapted to operational risk.

Or, you can ask your friendly neighborhood boy scout about being prepared. In 2010 the American Red Cross (ARC) debuted the new wilderness and remote first aid course that incorporates scenario-based learning for managing emergencies. The design allows everyone from the young to medical doctors to learn from experience and make the best decisions based on a logical understanding of causes, current situation, and similar future situations.

Jeffrey Pellegrino, of Kent State University in Ohio, was the lead developer of the wilderness and remote first aid course for the ARC. As he looks at learning needs, he stresses that although the tools and situations are different between the wilderness and the corporate world, the cross-over in lessons can be significant. "The biggest challenge is the same in both: communication. Working remotely (electronically or physically) complicates matters because of time lags and assumptions about what is happening. That is why documentation during every scenario is key; it establishes a common language, prioritizes needs, and helps organize resources between participants."

Financial companies can also benefit from other advantages of using scenarios in operational risk management:

"Besides having a common language, real-world scenarios (versus table-top or computer-generated ones) allow participants to gain appreciation of complex human factors which can change outcomes dramatically. One exercise we devised creates a scenario to test the ability of people to evaluate a current emergency and respond to risks while anticipating cascading issues. Another exercise simulates a scenario with competing priorities to see the participants' reaction and ability to proceed with the logical consequences. They then have the opportunity to recalibrate and deal with issues again.

"We came to stress the scenario approach because of its value in various learning approaches, such as experiential learning. This process helps improve how people respond to decision-making in emergencies, especially when under stress and time pressures, by providing feedback and forcing them to project further into the future. The process documents participants' abilities as well as detecting organizational holes—and is also a fun way to learn."

Improving cost/benefit balance

Second, in improving the cost/benefit of operational risk management. The decades-old answer to improving cost/benefit, from industries ranging from telecom to shipbuilding and from discrete manufacturing to distribution, is to dig down to the roots of how business processes work. **Clarifying business processes not only reveals risks, but also provides understanding to enhance processes—reducing risk *and* costs.** An excellent book on this topic is Philip Crosby's *Quality is Free.*[8] In his book, Crosby explains how improving quality (reducing the risk that quality objectives will not be achieved) saves cost and thus pays for itself.

Refining process analysis

Third, in refining process analysis. Process analysis has many benefits, including the creation of more insightful risk categories by developing classifications based on severity, detection, and prevention—as used in hospitals or electric utilities—and by finding root causes that can drive smarter fixes and by creating more predictive key risk indicators (KRIs) that are directly linked to key performance indicators (KPIs).

For example, a performance objective might be that 100 widgets are shipped on quality, on time and in budget. In this case, the risk is the likelihood that something will go wrong in the system resulting in a failure to ship the 100

---

[8] Crosby, Philip. (1979), *Quality is Free.* (New York: McGraw-Hill). In 1995, Crosby wrote *Quality is Still Free.* However, the title of the original book is pithier, and makes the point in itself.

widgets as expected, and the impact of that failure. The process analysis discipline brings a toolbox that includes many tools for finding and fixing risks in such business processes.

Lessons from risk response

In responding to risks, a common topic in financial services today is developing better controls. There is a tendency to look to controls on financial statement preparation and to seek a similar approach to managing operational risk—that is, to 'lock it down' to protect against discrete events, e.g. access violations. However, one lesson learned from other industries is that not everything can be controlled. Even in an industry such as pharmaceuticals, which is heavily controlled, there are still recalls. Instead, the more successful answer for operational risk is to look at the *system* and **take necessary actions to prevent and prepare for situations**.

Consider medical practice. Here process details, analysis, systems and culture are also key concerns. Jim Bagian, professor of engineering practice at The University of Michigan, is an engineer who is a medical doctor, an astronaut, and a member of the National Academy of Engineering and the Institute of Medicine. He is also the co-author of a 2010 study on methods for improving outcomes in medical care at Department of Veterans Affairs (VA) hospitals. With great passion, Professor Bagian describes the need to understand sources of risk and what works: "You go to hospitals and find professionals who do procedures differently on the same floor because that is what those individuals learned where they trained, not because someone did a head-to-head comparison to find what is better.

"In our VA study, we found that understanding what is better and turning that into decision guides, checklists in some cases, for evaluating conditions and structuring responses clearly improves communication among health care providers and results in better outcomes. This was part of a program called Medical Team Training. The 74 facilities in the training program experienced an 18% reduction in annual mortality, compared with a 7% decrease among the 34 facilities that had not yet undergone training."[9]

---

[9] An abstract can be found at **bit.ly/edOAvw**.

He found a few key features which created big benefits, and which we can adapt to risk response in financial services:

- "People are safe in reporting incidents and not punished when they report through the 'safety side', as opposed to the management side. However, we don't establish an entirely blame-free culture. Intentionally unsafe acts, criminal acts, drink or drugs have to be addressed. The relevant authorities—in our case, Congress and the labor unions—also have to get on board with this.

- "We provide tools for good, systems-based investigation, looking for specific root causes. In the old days, it was 'tell the nurse to be more careful'. We needed something better. We needed to specifically identify and understand the root causes, so as to make prudent changes that yielded sustainable improvements. We needed systems-based solutions to improve outcomes.[10]

- "We were clear on our goal at all times—in our case, that no patient should be inadvertently harmed while under our care.

- "We focused on the system, on designing approaches *into* the system to catch errors. For example, software that checks dosage amounts for appropriate ranges (rather than relying on personal vigilance).

- "We stressed the need for the right tool for the job. No 'silver bullets'."

In short, there are many factors to integrate into your response: physical, environmental, and personal. If we don't take them all into account in our risk management, then the chances of reaching our goal aren't good. The reason we are here is to provide safe and effective care for the patient—that is sustainable value."

In financial services, the basic types of operational threats can be grouped as 'natural', 'malicious', 'accidental', 'business activity' and 'agency'. Only some can be meaningfully controlled (and only some of those monitored). Crisis managers, lifeguards, hotels, air transportation, electric utilities, medical practice, oil and gas, and manufacturers all expend significant effort on detection and then effective response to contain the impact of a chain of cascading events. Proven approaches from a range of industries can also help reduce risk to outcomes in financial services operations.

---

[10] For more information on the VA root cause process, see **1.usa.gov/fP23E0**.

Bringing it Together

In closing, hopefully you will have noticed two points.

First, that **risk to operations in financial institutions is in general more similar to operational risk in other industries than it is to credit or market risk**.

Second, the emphasis on attention to detail in finding and fixing risks to operations. If this is an overwhelming thought, pause and take a breath. It's not that difficult. It really just **means *knowing the business***.

This is not an unreasonable expectation for any business line, functional or geographic area executive.

It also doesn't mean that you personally need to know every detail, just like the CEO doesn't. It does mean that you need to partner with business leaders to share appropriate methods and tools so that they have a structured, detailed understanding that enables them to reduce risk to performance objectives and comply—whether that is protecting against loss from accidents or malicious acts, or taking advantage of opportunities. In this way, both the CEO and you can be confident that the details are well understood and *actively managed*. By applying the right methods and tools, you can dramatically reduce the time it takes to make this happen.

Part 1.
Evaluating Risk

Finding and understanding risks to operations is the focus of this first part of the book. This includes understanding the dynamics of the environment in which the institution operates, the capabilities of the enterprise that is the financial institution, the interaction of the environment and capabilities as they play out in scenarios or situations of unfolding chains of events, and the warning signs of those unfolding events that should be watched to avoid cascading problems. This part of the book will introduce a systematic process for taking these steps to help you be more efficient and effective in finding and understanding risks.

1.1. Lighting up 'Dark Corners'

"In complex organizations, the operational risk manager must coordinate across all areas of the business to ensure risks are identified, measured in terms of the amount and severity of worst-case outcomes, and that plans are designed to prevent them. Board oversight, executive leadership and employee engagement across the business are required."

— *Karen Osar, board member of Webster Financial Corporation*

Regulators say: 'Banks need to better see in "dark corners".' Operational risk leaders ask: 'How can we avoid "surprises"?' Shareholders and board members facing a changing business environment seek risk management that improves return relative to risk. As I speak with ops risk executives, most express frustration and a sense that there must be a better way than just trudging through their daily challenges.

Practical experience in risk and operations suggests that **shifting to a more performance-driven, systematic approach to risk management can better meet shareholder expectations and helps meet compliance requirements**.

To shift to that performance focus, the operational risk management leader needs to strengthen the three basic ingredients in any productive activity— people, process and technology. To be more basic, it means *clarity* in terms so people can communicate easily, *effectiveness* in *framework* (including process) so they can get the job done, and *efficiency* in tools/technology so they can get the job done faster and easier.

Tools are best used in the context of a framework. This is true for any activity, whether for repairing a car or knitting a scarf.

There are a number of frameworks for risk management. With similarities and differences, frameworks can make life easier for practitioners. The more complete frameworks for management include these elements:

- what to do: process model steps

  - management practices

  - input–output tables

- what to measure: goals and metrics tables

- who does it: Responsible, Accountable, Consulted, Informed (RACI) tables

- how to measure and progress: maturity models or agreed upon procedures

- glossary.

Two groups of benefits come from using frameworks. First, there are design benefits. They are developed by teams with a range of perspectives (sometimes across industries and countries); are refined by peer review; come with supporting guidance and mapped to other frameworks and standards; and have a user community for help, training and periodic updates. Second, there are use benefits. They are flexible for tailoring to enterprise needs, but provide a defined measuring stick; are systematic to avoid gaps; improve communications clarity (internally, and to partners, regulators and shareholders); and add genuine credibility. In short, they save time and money.

A key element of a good framework is a risk management process cycle. To guide our selection and use of tools, this book is partly organized around taking you through the steps of this cycle; the following figure, and progressive variants of it, will recur throughout the book.

As one regulator observed: "This can be used for anything, right?" Yes, it can. It applies equally well to any type of risk to operations, whether to product, process, IT, facilities, people, intellectual property, reputation—anything. The cycle offered here is based on a long history of use in professional disciplines and industries (including several areas of financial institutions). This makes it valuable for two reasons—it draws on a record of success, and it makes it easier to communicate with colleagues from various backgrounds in managing risk to operations (and strategy).

Risk to operations management cycle

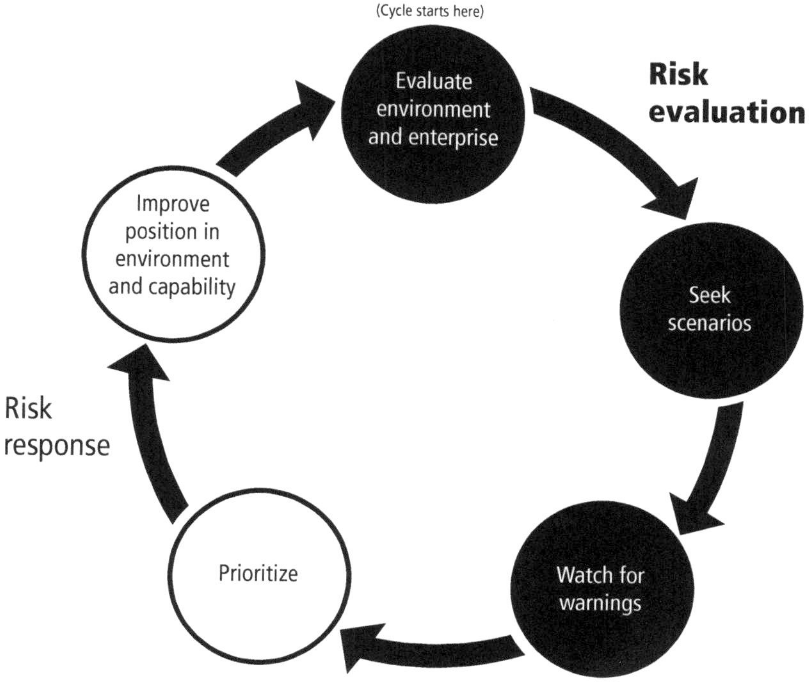

Figure 1

The process in this framework includes both evaluating and responding to risk. Evaluation steps are shown in the black circles; response steps in white. Bringing both together is the first step toward getting more business value from risk management. Starting with the topmost circle and moving clockwise:

- *Evaluate the environment and enterprise* is about the environment (economic, competitive, market, political, regulatory, social, technology, natural) in which an enterprise, product or process operates. The enterprise capabilities are those in product, process, IT and other areas of the institution that work together to achieve objectives.

- *Seek scenarios* illuminates how situations unfold in the environment and enterprise that can impact objectives.

- *Watch for warnings* looks for signs that the potential scenarios are unfolding.

- *Prioritize* uses the warning information to help select projects from the range of options that optimize risk–return performance and balance cost and benefit.

- *Improve position in environment and capability* designs and implements solutions to strengthen capabilities to earn return from taking risk; reposition away from danger; reshape the environment; or some combination of these. Improving capability includes oversight, management, controls and core business process. As the cycle continues, the new state of environment exposure and enterprise capability is evaluated and the cycle continues.

The speed at which the cycle spins will depend on the speed at which real-world situations unfold. Yet the risk leader need not be a passive victim of too-rapid events. Instead, each step in the cycle also points to the value of preparation so as to be ready to respond when a warning rings. In such a situation, the inner react loop is followed.

The risk management cycle addresses the 'normal' situation when time is available to build capability and/or reposition in the environment. When warnings ring, then rapid reaction is required.

Risk to operations management cycle

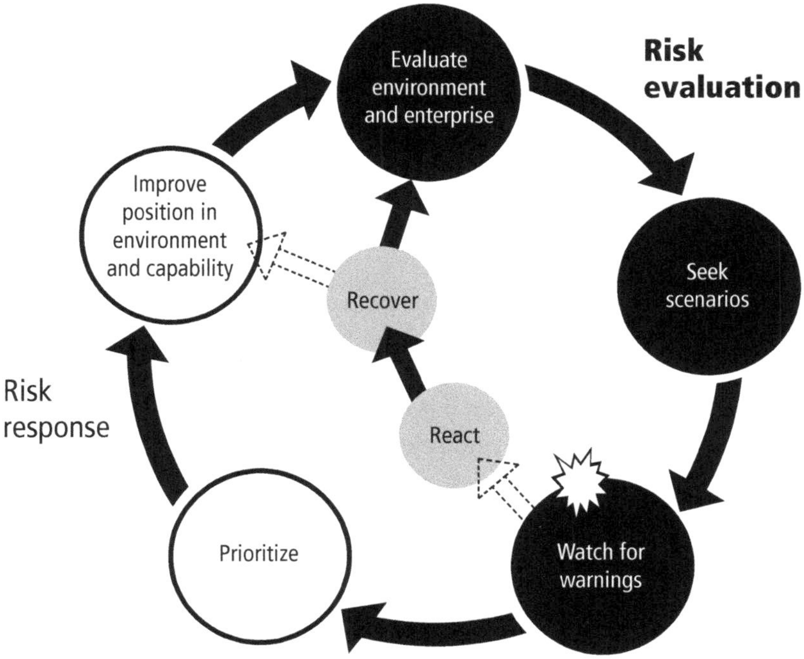

Figure 2

- *React* immediately implements pre-planned and other actions to contain, reduce or stop an unfolding chain of events.

- *Recover* begins when the cascading chain of events has been sufficiently stopped and the damaged capability can begin its journey back to 'normal' or 'steady state'. Depending on the extent of the damage, this may be relatively quick and with current resources (reversing a trade or resetting failed equipment) or more extensive (fire, earthquake, flood, fraud investigations, diagnoses and fixes) requiring new resources to be prioritized. In either case, the full risk evaluation and response cycle is resumed as the enterprise seeks to continually improve performance within its environment.

Speed is again prominent, based on the real-world speed of the unfolding situation, reaction and recovery.

The chapters that follow address each of the steps.

> *"The business press and the global press regularly tell us about preventable disasters, or lesser adverse events that affect reputations, profitability and even lives. Risk management is a tool to systematically identify what could go wrong, to what degree and how could it hurt us, and then to determine how to manage, mitigate or eliminate the risk. In corporations increasingly governed by managers with specialized expertise in manufacturing, logistics, supply chains, human resources etc, only a well-organized collaborative effort can succeed in evaluating risks so that they can be managed."*
>
> — *Karen Osar*

These three steps in risk evaluation will help answer common questions such as: Why are there so many 'surprises'? Is it all really the fault of 'unknown unknowns'? Are these situations really unknown to everyone or just to some institutions or some people in an institution? How do we get ahead of what the auditors or examiners will find next? How do we get more business value from all the resources spent on compliance?

Key concepts in these steps

The business objective of operational risk evaluation is to improve risk-adjusted return through better decisions based on a more complete understanding of risk to business operations. In financial terms, that means better risk-adjusted return on capital overall and individual investments in the institution. The *test* of the quality of risk evaluation is whether all the risks have been identified and understood.

Risks *cannot* be evaluated if we don't know they exist. Turning the lights on is doable because there are not many risks (at least root causes) that are new in the world. A risk might be new to a certain executive, business team, or even company, and yet well-known to many other people. A key task (and opportunity) is always to find the people who already know about the risk, and engage that learning in your risk management process, starting with risk evaluation.

Achieving better outcomes more efficiently and effectively is much easier with a focus on key points, briefed below and elaborated in ensuing chapters:

- Take a systems view of risk—the environment and enterprise capabilities. Scenarios are your central tool for understanding situations in time.

- Take a prospective, not a retrospective, view of risk evaluation.

- Understand the environment better than competitors. This is a requirement in strategy and operations. It's also a requirement in managing risk to your strategy and operations.

- Understand the business. A deep understanding of how it works is essential to finding and fixing risks before they cause damage, and to using your capabilities to take advantage of opportunities in a changing environment.

- Look for change. Change brings threats and opportunity.

- Find the person who already knows—few risks are truly new in the world.

- Identify the right performance measures and data.

- Select the right tool (approaches, methods, techniques) for the job. Maturing organizations need more efficient tools to be effective more easily.

- Relentlessly ask, 'What if?', 'When?' and 'How long?' Bring together the understanding of the environment and how the business works through robust scenarios to understand how to seize opportunities and guard against loss.

- Be honest. Rigorously check for bias. Markets, shareholders, competitors, customers and regulators will find flaws if you don't. Understand causes and types of bias and root them out before they hurt the business and make you look foolish.

- Be vigilant. Watch for warning signs in the environment, capability weakness and outcomes. Minimize lag time and static to create meaningful early warning indicators.

- Drive risk evaluation to improve business performance. Focusing on real performance should also cover the more narrow compliance exercise.

Digging into and applying these points will be our trip through the rest of Part 1:

1.2 – Know the Business: Evaluating the Environment and the Enterprise

1.3 – The Right Tool for the Right Risk Type

1.4 – Seeking Scenarios: Providing More Power to See—the 'Why' and 'What'

1.5 – Creating More Robust Scenarios More Easily—the 'How'

To begin our walkthrough of the performance-focused and systematic risk management cycle, we start with the external environment into which your institution sells offerings, and the enterprise capabilities used to create, sell and deliver those offerings.

1.2. Know the Business: Evaluating the Environment and the Enterprise

Risk to operations management cycle

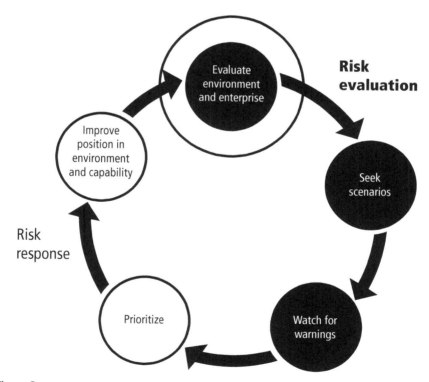

Figure 3

Risk management begins by understanding the business, including the dynamics of the environment and the enterprise capabilities used to survive and thrive in its environment.

The external environment shapes the risk profile

Institutions don't operate in isolation. Operational processes are not static and unaffected by events outside the walls of a branch or data center.

For example in a workshop with operational risk managers, real-life examples of risks to operations emerging from dynamic environments were shared:

- social unrest in an area normally deemed safe, requiring rapid protection of employees and physical assets
- competitors enhancing their products, prompting calls for fast response
- technological advances in mobile platforms that inadvertently open new routes to fraud and money laundering
- changes in jobless rates
- earthquakes in Japan forcing an institution to address its own needs and those of customers with supply chains linked to Japan
- moves by a country to prevent data from leaving its country (including data hosted there unrelated to customers in that country)
- espionage
- ever-changing regulations.

There are several reasonably established approaches for classifying environmental conditions. Categories include: political (including legal and country-specific), economic, competitive, market, regulatory, social, technological and natural. They can be further grouped by the actor: employee, contractor, customer, government, competitor, partner/supply chain/extended enterprise and other external party (including malicious ones). Actors have attributes, such as whether they are internal or external, that reflect their access or capability in a situation.

Too often, factors are not fully evaluated for their risk because they affect multiple areas of an institution or the effect on operations is not immediately clear. As is described more in the chapters on scenario analysis, the environment analysis is foundational. For now, two tips:

1. Be aware of available analyses of environmental factors (from commercial and government sources) and the need to evaluate implications for your operating environment and capabilities.

2. Compare notes. Talk to your strategy, marketing, sales, business continuity, currency trading, information technology, country (if a multi-country institution), security, legal, government relations leaders and more. Learn what they are tracking and the implications for you. Drive action together.

Your enterprise shapes your ability to bounce back from adversity and seize opportunity

Once there is a view of the business environment, we turn to how the enterprise (the institution) fits into the environment. The head of operational risk at one global bank told me: "I want to hire people who know the business." The enterprise evaluation considers the institution's products, processes, capabilities and culture. Just like a sports team before a big game, the question is the extent to which it can 'take it' and 'give it' on offense or defense. These capabilities can be competitively benchmarked.

It is important to grasp that an **enterprise is part of a *system***. A system is a bounded group of inputs, processes and outputs. It can be simple or complex. This is crucial in looking at environments such as programmed trading, weather patterns, road traffic, customer savings rates, information technology failures, safety in chemical refineries and so many more environments. This system itself is also interconnected with customers and other institutions. Systems that are too 'lean' have too little margin for error and too much risk. Systemic risk must therefore always be a significant concern.

It's not about piece-parts. As we'll see later, in the section on scenario and dependency analysis, failure to properly identify system boundaries and elements leads to large losses (sub-prime mortgages and trade processing being just two examples).

Bridging from the external environment to the enterprise starts with the business strategy that seeks to improve risk-adjusted return within an environment. For purposes of an operational analysis, we assume the environment is a given and thus that strategy shapes the operational situation—leading to increasing or decreasing risk in operations. This is why it is important to engage with the strategy, M&A, new products, marketing, geographic, human resources and other teams involved with change resulting from working to operationalize strategic adjustments to the environment. Engaging these others gives operational risk leaders earlier visibility to strategy changes that affect operational risk and, more proactively, the opportunity for operational risk leaders to provide an end-to-end view of risk to operations to inform strategic decisions.

Through that dialogue, the operational risk leader can better understand risk to *business objectives*—official plans, personal objectives and reports. What do they already have documented that can speed your effort? As you work through your analysis, you will likely generate insights to share back with them—demonstrating your value and furthering the mutual benefit of the coordination.

Making it personal: knowing objectives and knowing the business

You might be surprised by how quickly your colleagues will seek your assistance when dealing with risk to their personal objectives or formal roles related to management of risk to the institution.

Tool tip: formalizing roles and responsibilities

"Without the 'A', there is no way the objective will be accomplished!" The 'A' is for the 'accountability' that is needed in any project. For any project or any task within a project, there should be one and only one accountable role. Other roles are people who are 'responsible', 'consulted' and 'informed'. Together, these are described as the 'RACI' roles.

A tool to help understand and improve role assignments is the RACI chart. A RACI chart has columns for each organizational role, rows for each task in a project, and each cell is labeled with an R, A, C or I to indicate the role. RACI charts are used in a wide variety of situations. For operational risk in financial institutions, the tables that are the closest starting point are found in ISACA's *Risk IT* Based on the COBIT (*Risk IT*) framework (**www.isaca.org/riskit**).

To tailor the generic *Risk IT* RACI charts to your institution: Adjust for 1) your organizational structure (business line, functional areas, geographic regions), 2) organization design (centralized, decentralized), and 3) roles appropriate for financial services operational risk, such as those described above in the section on integrating with enterprise-wide risk management.

Note: There are several variations on the RACI chart. Some add the role 'support'. However, that is a bit wimpy. 'Support' is too often just a way to avoid responsibility. Well-run organizations are looking for responsibility. As a former boss asked me when a decision had to be made: "Are you on the boat or off the boat?"

When personal business objectives are stated in terms of product revenue, growth, customer acquisition or retention, process efficiency, customer satisfaction and such, this quickly leads to specific product offerings and the business processes that support them (and then the technology and technology management process on which the business depends).

Digging into these brings to light any problems in the end-to-end processes that may have resulted from acquisitions, quick fixes, complexity in supporting technology or immaturity in process management. All of these introduce risk. All of these are opportunities for improvement that not only reduce risk of failure, but also save time and cost in processing transactions and meeting customer needs. The cost of managing risk to improve quality should be recovered in the savings from fewer problems and more revenue opportunity.

Tip: Quality, like risk, can be 'free'. However, too many quality programs get bogged down in process. Don't let this happen to your risk program. Use this book to keep it focused on delivering better business outcomes. This both embeds risk management more deeply into the institution and makes you look like a hero.

"The purpose of operational risk management is not to observe risk levels passively but to understand the root causes of risks and actively work to mitigate them. The power to understand risks and actually address them comes at the level of individual organizational units—where you can assess the quality of the processes and controls in place."

— **Ron Dietz, chairman of the audit and risk committee of the board of directors, Capital One Financial**

An end-to-end view

Understanding the business includes having an end-to-end view of a business activity (business line, product, process) and how it works to grow profitable revenue (and the characteristics of problems that put revenue at risk). Two ways to understand business process may be found in *scope* and *dependencies*:

- Scope—having a clear view of the whole of an 'end-to-end' business process. **Scope is in the context of the system—where a process begins and ends so that key aspects aren't missed that would lead to errors in all the risk evaluation steps that follow**. 'Death by silo' means that no one has a view of upstream or downstream process sufficient to understand the full impact of the risk involved—whether terrorist activities or sub-prime mortgage origination in California.

> **Tip:** To assess business value, understand customer touch points in the revenue-generating processes. Here you'll find operational risks to revenue that grab the attention of business leaders (not just compliance issues that are seen as merely adding cost without value).

- Dependencies—the range of people and processes that enable a business to operate to expected performance objectives. This includes trained people, IT (applications, middleware, servers, storage, networking) and facilities. Understanding the dependencies of your business on this system of people and processes, and the infrastructure that this all runs on (including the management and infrastructure which in turn undergirds this), is vital, and can be achieved with dependency analysis.

Dependency analysis is exactly what the name implies—it illustrates what depends on what, usually in graphical form. Dependency analysis is one of a variety of root-cause techniques that illustrate how capabilities (such as two application software programs) are connected. It's a bit like 'the knee bone is connected to the thigh bone' game. It helps you see what matters in making a process in a system work.

Versions of dependency diagrams are already in use elsewhere in your institution showing how people, data, IT and other resources are connected. Process flow, data flow, user-interaction, architecture—whatever the name, they can help you. This is also an opportunity to invite those people to join the team to improve the speed and quality of risk evaluation.

'Talk the T'

A starting point for dependency analysis is the T-diagram. This can be helpful for briefing executive sponsors prior to a scenario analysis workshop or for opening the workshop. As the T-diagram is generic, it can be used as a basic illustration before team members share their diagrams used by their areas of the institution.

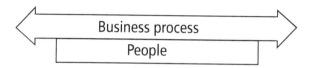

Figure 4

Start with the horizontal line by defining the business process that supports the products sold by that business team. This could be a financial closing process, consumer home insurance policy application, loan application, or transferring money between consumer accounts (especially in more complicated situations such as across acquired banks). The process could be 'straight through' or comprised of sub-processes and/or multiple software applications (more on that later). In scoping risk, it is crucial to understand the ends of the top of the 'T' and how they connect to other processes. Again, in the sub-prime loan mess, the process view was often scoped too narrowly, so the entire risk in the system wasn't clearly visible. The result was bad. The first dependency is people, which could be multiple roles of people. As few processes are still manual, we now dig a bit into the 'stack' of information technology on which the products, people and process depend.

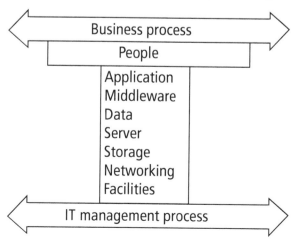

Figure 5

Next, look at the vertical line of the 'T' to document all the information technology and physical infrastructure on which the process depends. In reality, there is more detail in the vertical and there may be multiple vertical lines because a process depends on multiple software application stacks.

- To help you find gaps more easily, give extra attention to variations from documented processes and the controls in the processes. These include variations due to error, innocent expediting (which can cause problems), and formal exceptions. The point is to understand what happens, good or bad, when the process is not followed. A higher percentage of exceptions (formal and informal) is a flag indicating the need to fix the core process. Smaller institutions should look for fast payback activities, such as converting from manual to automated controls.

- These stacks can get a little foggy when cloud or virtualization techniques are used—but there are ways to handle that. For example, guidance on cloud computing risk evaluation and response is available from many sources such as ISACA (**www.isaca.org**), the Cloud Security Alliance (**www.cloudsecurityalliance.org**) and the Shared Assessments Program (**www.sharedassessments.org**). Cloud risk management is an excellent example of the need for a robust, process-based approach to risk management. Checklists are overwhelmed with the changes in cloud. By contrast, scenario and dependency analyses excel at understanding change.

- Outsourcing (especially off-shoring) of application development also creates extra risks, especially if a business objective is flexibility to beat competitors and/or meet customer needs more quickly. Off-shoring tends to slow down product management and reduce agility.

The point is that stepping through the risk to operations makes it easier for various roles to understand how they affect each other, to learn the ways in which they can make immediate improvements through daily actions, and to design shared approaches to better reduce risk. This approach is not only educational, but forges a tighter bond between people.

Two tips are particularly helpful to get the most from dependency analysis:

1. Engage 'the business'. Bring together relevant roles from business lines, functions and regions. Use this as an opportunity for people to understand how their actions impact others and avoid the 'throw it over the wall' syndrome. In many cases, one team is causing problems for another. These can be fixed immediately to provide more business benefit.

2. Take advantage of the structured walkthrough to understand exactly how a process really works. Often, people will come to a dependency analysis session with diagrams that are like puzzle pieces. It is likely that not all of the diagrams are current, that varying terminology and symbols are used, or there are gaps. This session can provide significant value to the business well beyond risk management in helping everyone to understand how the pieces really work on a daily basis.

A bit of Basel

Evaluating the environment and enterprise with these approaches and tools should both improve business performance and address the Basel requirement of evaluating the business environment and internal control (BEIC) as one of the "four fundamental elements" in quantitative analysis. The introduction of section 676 of *A Revised Framework* states: "In addition to using loss data, whether actual or scenario-based, a bank's firm-wide risk assessment methodology must capture key business environment and internal control factors that can change its operational risk profile. These factors will make a bank's risk assessments more forward-looking, more directly reflect the quality of the bank's control and operating environments, help align capital assessments with risk management objectives, and recognize both improvements and deterioration in operational risk profiles in a more immediate fashion."

It is particularly notable that the Basel Committee seeks to use this element to make risk assessments "more forward-looking".

Summary

In evaluating the enterprise, an approach was suggested to take both a) an end-to-end view of the product process and b) the dependencies that must execute to deliver that product, through processes. In other words, adopt an approach to get a genuinely accurate and comprehensive understanding of how the business works. This is done in the context of the external environment, so as to understand the sources and nature of changes that provide threats or opportunities to the business products and processes.

If the institution already has high-quality product- and process-improvement initiatives in place, it is relatively easy to work through existing documents to spot process-related risks (many of which will already be identified as part of improvement plans). If this doesn't already exist, it needs to be done. If done efficiently, one analysis can generate bonus benefits, saving time and money for multiple teams seeking business improvements to grow profitable revenue.

Looking forward

In moving forward, this environment and enterprise capability (including products, process and dependencies insight) come together to create descriptions or stories about what could happen—the 'What ifs?' This will provide a measure of the risk (frequency and impact) that can be compared to what the board of directors defines as acceptable risk to the institution overall, and the risk that they allocate to each business line, functional or geographic unit.

Specifically, the dependency analysis provides a road map that describes how root causes in a system can cascade. This will be used in the seek scenarios and subsequent steps.

1.3. The Right Tool for the Right Risk Type

"In evaluating risk, a big problem that I see is that people aren't using the right tool for the job. Dashboards are important for status, often including after-the-fact data. However, they rarely give early warning and don't fix problems. We need support systems that look into the operations of the institution, provide early warnings and point us to causes, so we can fix problems promptly."

— *Humphrey Polanen, founding director of Heritage Bank of Commerce*

In public presentations and private workshops, people often ask: 'You've mentioned so many tools, how do I know what to use for what?' A diagram can help. Figure 6 maps the risk space to tool types for both finding and evaluating risks to operations.

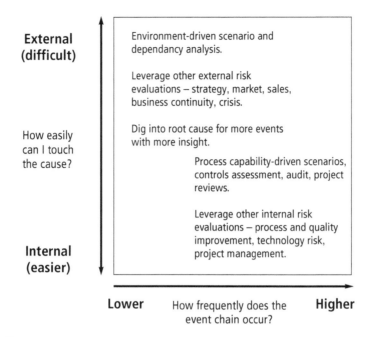

Figure 6

The right tool for the right job is just as important here as when building a house, fixing a car or cooking a meal. For example, many institutions attempt to evaluate externally originating, non-process risks (such as hazards) with control assessments. This helps a little—like chopping carrots with a dull paring knife. But, control assessments are *not* well suited for addressing external, non-process risks that are usually in dynamic threat environments (such as adverse weather or a malicious attacker). Further, control assessments *assume* that the root cause is already well understood and that controls (where possible) were properly designed and implemented. Back to the cooking analogy, control assessments aren't as helpful as taking a scenario approach with a scenario generator looking at a range of possibilities—like a food processor that can more quickly chop a range of foods at once.

The tool guidance diagram simply asks two obvious questions about what you already know and don't know:

1. How frequently do I see events with clear root causes? This not only concerns 'How much data do I have?' but also 'Is the data insightful in terms of understanding how bad it is and how to fix it because it is real *root*-cause information?' Having more data points, especially more root-

cause data, means that more quantitative and process-based tools are appropriate. Fewer data points or data without root causes means that more logical analysis tools and discovery-oriented tools will be appropriate.

2. How easily can I touch the root cause? A root cause that is easier to touch is a root cause that is more readily accessible and controllable by the institution or at least a business process. This means that process quality and improvement tools (such as business process reengineering [BPR] from Michael Hammer and James Champy, total quality management [TQM] from W. Edwards Deming, and SixSigma from Motorola) are appropriate starting points.

CAUTION:

- If the root cause is more difficult to touch (access and control), then tools are needed to understand those root causes, how they unfold in a scenario, how to watch for warning signs and how to prepare.

- BPR, TQM, SixSigma and many other approaches have risen and fallen through waves of popularity. Implementations of these approaches too often struggled because they lacked focus or ability to coordinate with related initiatives. Risk management can overcome typical pitfalls because risk management is intended to pinpoint root cause and prioritize actions that work together to build capability, and/or reposition within or reshape an environment to reduce risk to operational objectives.

In addition, maturity of the risk management process needs to be considered in two ways:

1. First, certain tools expect inputs from other tools. For example, as noted above, it is premature to jump to control self-assessments without first understanding root cause. This is necessary to determine the placement of a control, which is in turn necessary to design a control, which is, lastly, necessary to implement and maintain a control. Jumping ahead in tool use can waste resources and give a false sense of confidence.

2. Second, to help select, or better use, the next tool. As controls, risk indicators and other data become available, that information can be used to improve the prioritize step of the risk management cycle.

This simple approach of matching the tools with risk types has the potential to save significant time and energy in risk evaluation and

response planning. Many tools have long-proven track records in risk-related disciplines inside and outside of financial services. Seek out your colleagues in your institution, in your community or professional associations to learn what is helping them be successful.

This is important for more than just discovery. It is also important for creating the business case. **When key risks—and their responses—are missed when building the business case, the business case understates the benefits from the actions taken (and resources needed).** Further, it may mean that sub-optimal responses are taken because the responses are not designed to reduce as many threat types as possible with as efficient a set of actions as possible.

For example, when a business case is focusing on reducing big fraud risks, it might leave out (and thus understate) the benefits of reducing loss from many higher frequency, moderate or low-loss process errors. A high occurrence number multiplied by even a low-loss-per-occurrence number can still result in big cost savings.

In another example, if a business case only looks at one 'event', it can fail to fully capture the impact costs of the preceding and following events and all their consequences. Reputation damage is a consequence of upstream events (and losses) such as data breach or fraud made public. Avoiding that loss, and worse, are benefits to include in the business case.

Key points

- Use the right tool for the right risk type.

- Tools can be selected based on how easy it is to see the root cause, how frequent the root cause is seen and the maturity of the risk management process.

- The right tools not only help to better find risks, but also capture full costs and benefits for business cases to fix risks.

1.4. Seeking Scenarios: Providing More Power to See—the 'Why' and 'What'

Risk to operations management cycle

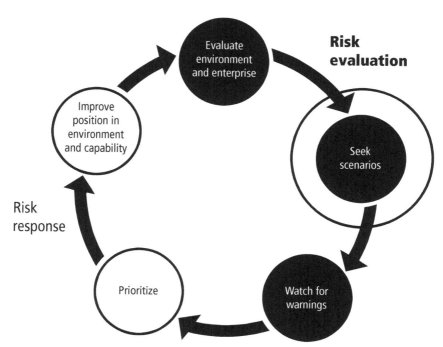

Figure 7

"Scenario analysis is pretty straightforward once you understand the bounds of the dynamic system and the risks being taken and what are the operational risks. The scenarios should tell a full story of how risks develop and cascade through a system to impact real operations."

— **Rick Sergel, director and chair of compensation committee of State Street Corporation**

When I'm asked, "How do I better see in 'dark corners'?", I reply, "What are you doing now?" Too often, the answer I hear is about putting together some sort of risk list. Then I ask: "How well are you engaging the business and getting insight?" Again, the answer is often not confident. Scenario analysis is the key tool for overcoming this. It provides more insight and better engages the business.

Scenario analysis brings together the information from an enterprise's environment and capability evaluations to tell a story about the risks to performance it faces, to provide insight on how it depends on IT, and to assist in detecting and understanding unfolding events that will affect it, as well as their likelihood and impact.[11] Because it tells a story, it is often referred to as a storyboard approach. In special features at the end of a motion picture, the director might be shown discussing the storyboard or pre-visualization for the film and insights gained and decisions made using the storyboard—before expensive filming began. In financial institutions, your colleagues may be using this approach for a range of purposes already. For example:

- creating user scenarios and mock-ups of software applications

- evaluating conditions that would lead to a change in the price of gold and currency prices

- devising likely responses to competitors with new products and markets

- assessing political changes in countries

- planning live business continuity exercises.

To get value from the time put into scenario analysis, it is critical to tell realistic, life-like stories. For example, a limited scenario is: 'How long does it take to get server *xyz* up after it fails?' A more robust version would be,

---

[11] Because risk terminology varies among professional disciplines, please note that in this book, 'likelihood' refers to qualitative, frequency counts and more sophisticated probability estimates. 'Frequency' is emphasized for both computational reasons and because of some psychological research that suggests that humans can more accurately respond to questions asking them to estimate frequency than likelihood or probability.

'How long does it take to resume supplying cash through ATMs if server *xyz* goes down during a regional blizzard due to part failure?' Similarly, a scenario of '$50M loss due to litigation *xyz*' is inadequate. Rather, a more complete scenario is: 'Product launch without full knowledge of state-specific variations in regulation, combined with inadequate training of new employees following acquisition, leads to compliance gaps, customer claims liability, and protracted negative publicity.' Life-like scenarios also provide more realistic input to stress testing.

Scenarios help understand how *events unfold*, cascade and have coincidence in a *system*. The storyboard-style scenario analysis discussed here is *not* the scenario analysis in the narrow sense used by some for compliance purposes such as 'long-tail testing'. The phrase '$10 million internal fraud' is not a complete story. Further, operational risk managers sometimes find themselves puzzling over the somewhat circular process of using thin (not life-like) scenarios to augment loss data in long-tail estimation and then go right to the limited data to check the reasonableness of the scenarios. Moving to more life-like, realistic scenarios as used by other disciplines inside and outside of the institution can overcome such circular problems.

More specifically, scenarios tell a story: actor, action, timing, object, indirect object, impact, consequence, and coincidence. Storyboards are used to touch a wide range of roles and objectives in the institution to reflect real events in real life.

Scenario snippets from workshops include:

1. an external actor, with fraudulent information, at a suburban branch, at the end of the business day on a deposit transaction to launder money

2. an external actor, with Trojan code, sent multiple times over a prolonged period at vulnerable servers to attack databases to secretly obtain data

3. an organized crime gang compromising employees in an offshore location, over a prolonged period to skim funds and/or gain intelligence on potential victims.

These are not fully developed scenarios, but show the variety. Looking at a range of threats from malicious, natural, accidental, business volume and agency problem sources to a range of targets/resources/assets (people, process, hardware, software, IT management processes, facilities, and more) has been termed an 'all-threats', 'all hazards' or 'all-risks' view. The point is to embrace a range of potential risks across business, functional and geographic lines (such as how the sub-prime mess involved multiple areas of an institution).

Event flow diagrams show how the dominos fall when events cascade through a system. They provide a view of *upstream and downstream events* from the starting point event. They can illustrate broad scenarios such as systemic risk across financial institutions, or smaller scenarios such as multiple breached controls that permit a rogue trader or executive (the 'agent') eager to 'make a number' act in a way that is not in the best interests of shareholders (the 'principal').[12] The next chapter includes an example.

If you're already worried about stimulating your team's creative juices to build life-like scenarios, never fear. Many tools can help. Some come from your strategy colleagues considering growth, complexity and the political landscape. Also, change creates risk. Change analysis tools look at environment, management and activity changes (more on this in the chapter on IT-related business risk). Scenarios also come from actual, test or audit failures in your institution or other companies. Don't forget that big problems can result from both big (flood) and little (server failure) issues. More idea-generation tools are available from your product management colleagues (more on this in the product management and fraud chapter).[12] The how-to of scenario analysis is the subject of the next chapter.

Key points

- Scenario analysis brings together information from the environment and enterprise capability evaluations to tell a story about the risks to the institution, gain insight on dependencies and the ability to detect cascades of unfolding events in a system.

- Tell realistic, life-like stories.

- Event-flow diagrams are the next step to documenting the logic of a scenario for better root-cause analysis and quantification.

---

[12] Appendix A of *A New Approach for Managing Operational Risk*, Revised, Society of Actuaries, 2010, provides a helpful discussion of the principal-agent problem.

1.5. Creating More Robust Scenarios More Easily—the 'How'

"Banks have historically been good at high-level process analysis because they have dedicated many hours to improving the efficiency of their many operational functions. But I think they are less familiar with, and therefore less proficient at, root-cause analysis—and the way that root cause has become critical to process improvement in recent years. Root-cause issues tend to be less immediately visible; it can require some digging to get to the roots. We need tools to make this analysis easier."

— *Mark Olson, former member, board of governors, of US Federal Reserve System Board of Governors*

Creating more revealing scenarios to see into dark corners and avoid nasty surprises happens through a series of workshops where people in multiple roles engage together to describe business performance objectives within a system— a process, its scope, the environment in which it operates, the dependencies on which it rests and what can go bump in the night. These workshops are highly efficient in creating valuable outputs if planned and managed well.

Planning to create workshop value

Start by building the right team for the scope of the scenario(s) being addressed. The scope may be a business line, product family, functional area or geographic area. Include experts on the environmental factors touching this scope, as well as experts who enable the outcomes (e.g. branch operations, IT, marketing).

Next, conduct interviews with the senior executive in charge of each relevant business line, function or region to explain the process, gather suggestions on areas of focus, understand current business and personal objectives, and ask for the appointment of a working representative from that business area to the workshop group.

> **Tip:** Having clearly defining *business objectives* is important to the workshop to ensure a focus on risks to those objectives, for reporting back with the results of the workshop, and for shaping business cases for improvement of the risks identified.

Once the right team is in place, two pre-work steps are encouraged.

Step 1

Find helpful information that already exists. Poll the team members to find information on root cause. Excellent sources include:

- Business environment. Competitive and market analyses point to the need for improvements in operations to stay competitive or take advantage of new opportunities. These are especially helpful as they can help the proactive risk manager get ahead of the business-planning process and engage business line leaders with ways to reduce risk to business operations performance.

- Business unit strategic and tactical plans. These include product, marketing, sales, delivery and support plans, along with the enabling financial and human resource plans. Specific plans can be associated with operational objectives; objectives have performance indicators and risks indicators (the latter reflecting the likelihood that performance will not meet objectives).

- Executive performance plans. These are the performance measures used for calculating compensation of business line, functional and regional executives. They help the risk manager in two ways. First, aligning risk management efforts with business performance objectives. Second, evaluating whether the compensation approach is aligned with the board of directors' risk-taking expectations (which should reflect both shareholder and regulatory expectations).

- Dependency information from maps of business process to information technology hardware and software (often called 'resources' or 'assets' by information technology [IT] teams) from business process improvement, architecture and service-level management.

- Business process gaps and needed improvements from requirements documents created by product management and software application development teams.

- Logs of failures and errors from automated monitoring tools that check business processes, software applications and IT resources (hardware and software). These tools accumulate mountains of detail on problems that cost time and effort.

- Internal and external loss data, especially data on true root (as opposed to proximate) cause and how the event chain unfolded. This includes post-incident reviews (PIRs) of previous situations where events unfolded into losses.

Step 2

Guide sub-teams in preparing the presentations for the workshop. A helpful approach is to organize the sub-teams into three groups: business analysis and strategy, business product and operations, and information technology. The content they prepare is discussed below. For now, the point is that it's helpful for each sub-team to work together to organize their existing information and collaborate on their workshop presentation in order to make the workshop with the full team more efficient. This will mean getting more quickly to the key issues, clearly defining how risks can unfold and designing insightful solutions to reduce risk to performance.

Conducting the scenario workshop for fun and value

With the team and pre-work in place, there are then eight steps in the typical scenario analysis workshop:

Step 1. Review and clarify the environment analysis.

Step 2. Review and clarify the enterprise capability analysis.

Step 3. Review the scenario format and approach.

Step 4. Create initial scenarios.

Step 5. Conduct a quick comparison of the scenarios created.

Step 6. Walk-through each scenario.

Step 7. Graphically illustrate the scenario and event flow.

Step 8. Add numbers with factor analysis.

Step 1

Review and clarify the environment analysis. Engage the workshop group! This section is best led by a sub-team from strategy, competitive and market analysis, regulatory affairs and information technology.

Step 2

Review and clarify the enterprise capability analysis. Engage the workshop group! This is best led by a sub-team from the unit around which the scope of the analysis is based. Key supporting functional areas should also be engaged (sales, information technology, business continuity and others) to present the 'picture' for the unit being discussed.

Step 3

Review the scenario format with the entire team: actor, action, timing, object, indirect object, impact, consequence, and coincident. Existing scenarios from the evaluation cycle are also reviewed to determine whether there are gaps in the content or conditions have changed. If this is the first time that the storyboard approach to scenario analysis has been used in your institution, there will be gaps to identify.

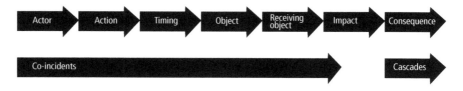

Figure 8

At this point, many workshops are nearing the end of the first day. The leader may wish to break the group into teams or have people work individually on the next step: *create initial scenarios.*

Step 4

Create initial scenarios. The leader distributes a scenario template on paper or in a word-processing document. The template helps avoid gaps in information. Create scenarios individually or in teams of two or three people. Each person should generate at least ten scenarios. With 20 people in a workshop, that provides a minimum of 200 starting points. **All steps in the scenario flows must be filled in to tell a life-like story.**

Tips:

Think broadly to capture *now* what would seem an obvious scenario later in a post-incident review.

Remember to look upstream and downstream from your starting point to see the cascade of events through a system.

The 'right' number of scenarios is driven by the complexity of your institution. Encourage participants to add scenarios until they notice overlap. Then just note the variations on the primary scenario page.

To spur creativity, use scenario generators, generic scenarios or other idea-generation techniques as appropriate.

Scenario generators

Scenario generators help solve the complaint of 'We can't imagine.' Scenario generators not only help generate potential scenarios but they make risk evaluation (and response) far more manageable. The total number of scenarios that could result out of a set of real-life factors can easily number in the thousands. Seeing large numbers, many organizations have given up and used a very small number without much diversity or depth. They are then surprised when something bad happens and call it an 'unknown unknown' or 'Black Swan'. This is an unfortunate and avoidable result.

In reality, the set of discrete factors at play in any risk is smaller and easier to identify. Further, they can a) be grouped into buckets by each of the scenario storyboard steps and b) be tracked back to more common root causes. This smaller number of factors is what is used to create a scenario-generator template. And there's a bonus: These factors for the scenario generator not only make it easier to create more insightful and complete scenarios, but will be later used to help identify high-value risk-response actions.

Scenario-generator templates must be tailored to the risks being considered in a workshop. This is done by adding or subtracting the factors for each stage of the scenario. For example, a template designed for risks to processing operations (such as the example below) can include the four Action, Action and Object threat sources listed—Malicious, Accidental, Natural and Business. However, if the template is to create scenarios for a trading process, then 'Agency' would also be included in the Actor, Action and Object/Threat categories. This is done to include situations where employees (not for malicious purposes) act in a manner inconsistent with the interests of shareholders—the principal-agent problem.

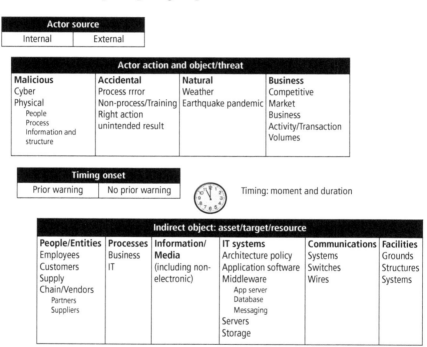

Figure 9

- Generic scenarios. Some best practices and guidance documents from professional organizations and government sources provide generic or example scenarios with which teams can begin their work. Some regulatory guidance specifically mentions aspects that should be included in scenarios. For example, the US FFIEC (**www.ffiec.gov**) *IT Examination Handbook for Business Continuity* specifically mentions that scenarios should consider that people cannot travel by air to a back-up location and to consider diversity in physical infrastructure, not just suppliers (who often share infrastructure with another provider). Among professional associations, ISACA's *Risk IT Practitioner Guide* has the most extensive list, with 72 generic scenarios. It is at **www.isaca.org/riskit**.

- Ideation techniques. A rich variety of techniques have been used to encourage group creativity in making the 'unknown, unknowns' known. Lists and descriptions of these are available from a range of sources. One respected source provides a list and descriptions that includes: Phillips 66 groups, brainstorming circle, reverse brainstorming, tear-down, 'and also', synetics, Gordon method, Delphi, and 'think tanks'. These and other techniques are listed and briefly described in appendices B and C of *New Products Management*, Ninth Edition, by C. Merle Crawford and Anthony Di Benedetto, (McGraw-Hill, 2008). These techniques should make scenario analysis fun! The leader can play video clips from action movies, television dramas or television situation comedies—these are stories that can spur creativity!

- Learn as a team. Workshops can help people immediately spot product and process problems that are low-hanging fruit to improve. To achieve this more easily, include a diversity of people who can both find and fix risks to return. Depending on the structure of the workshop, people and teams can work individually in the remainder of the afternoon and finish during an extended breakfast. If off-site, it could be part of evening 'homework', when people can think in a more relaxed way.

Step 5

Conduct a quick comparison of the scenarios created for: realistic covering of each step of the story; avoiding duplications; and relevance to the scope of this particular scenario. This can be done easily by simply having each group pass their scenarios to the next group in a circle. The peer review also starts to build confidence in the process and helps prepare for the next step.

Step 6

Full team walk-through of each scenario. Team members should add elements to the presented storyboard that make it real and relevant to their area. Each person answers the question: 'If this chain of events were initiated, how would my area be impacted?' The leader should be careful to gain agreement here. In some corporate cultures the leader might seek explicit agreement from each member that appropriate impacts are covered. Achieving group agreement here will be key to building a shared response plan and business case for whatever prevention and preparation actions are required.

> **Bonus:** To make clear the importance of seeing today what might be revealed in some future post-incident review, the team can discuss the institution's own post-incident reviews, public reviews from other institutions including media stories and legal investigations, and the lessons from other industries. For powerful material, a range of government agencies and industry associations maintain incident reviews on their websites. These include the Financial Services Information Sharing and Analysis Center (**www.fsisac.com**), the North American Electric Reliability Corporation (**www.nerc.com**), the US Chemical Safety Board (**www.csb.gov**; see especially their videos), and the US National Transportation Safety Board (**www.ntsb.gov**). The lessons of post-incident reviews tell us it is rare that no one really knew that the conditions were in place for something bad to occur. Take this lesson to heart. **Seek out people and information to fully understand a current situation and the way that events could unfold. Siloed or compartmentalized knowledge is the enemy to finding and fixing risks**.

Step 7

To more clearly capture the unfolding chains of events (especially in the more creative scenarios generated by the team), create an event-flow diagram to graphically illustrate the team's final view of the scenario.

The dots/nodes in the chart are described by:

- name
- ability to detect (that the event occurred)
- root(s)
- consequence(s)
- likelihood (probability or frequency)
- impact at this stage. Describing impact at each stage is valuable because is illustrates where to place controls that can prevent, reduce or stop the impact of an unfolding chain of events. It also provides benefit data for the business case to implement the fix.

The flows/arrows are described by:

- name

- business owner

- process group

- last revision date

- maturity rating of the process capability.

For example, Figure 10 describes a series of unfolding events that lead to a trading loss:

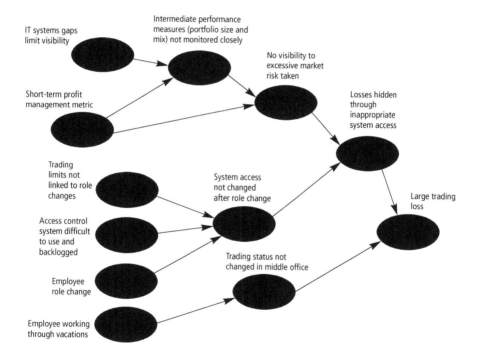

Figure 10

This diagram is an example of a piece of a chain of events. The flow could continue with damage to relationships that results in further revenue loss.

Step 8

Add numbers. Quantify the logic in the storyboards and supporting flows of unfolding events by assigning numerical weights to each of the factors and valuing the impacts at each stage of the unfolding chain. This is generally termed 'factor analysis'.

This process should be familiar from daily life.

Consider a sporting event like football or tennis. What is the probability a team or player will win? Both sports commentators and gamblers evaluate key conditions:

- the environment in which they are playing (temperature, altitude, surface [clay or grass—real turf or artificial])

- the environment that supports the players (coaching, equipment, medical care)

- the capabilities of players on the offense and defense.

Factor analysis should also be familiar from a range of other business analyses that need to structure human judgment:

- For example, in sales, factor analysis is used to verify sales forecasts, structuring based on stage of sales pipeline, product or sales regions.

- In product management it is used to evaluate information about new products or markets to determine whether to invest (or keep investing).

- The quality control/improvement and business-process-improvement disciplines have a variety of related techniques. In the quality improvement discipline, factor analysis is one of a number of root-cause techniques. It is often associated with 'fishbone' or Ishikawa diagrams (so named for Kaoru Ishikawa [1915–1989]). These diagrams depict root causes drawn in a way that looks a bit like the bones of a fish (the ribs being root-cause branches). These fishbone diagrams are a more basic version of the event flows described here. Fault tree analysis is another version. A range of other tools such as the '5 Whys' (asking 'why?' five times as a simple way to get to the root cause) are available from quality control approaches such as total quality management (TQM), Crosby's methods and SixSigma. These approaches combine objectives, processes, roles, tools and more.

- The information-security discipline has used this technique, so much so that several vendors have built the basic math into their software. A particularly robust example is found in the factor analysis of information risk (FAIR) method developed by Jack Jones. It is referenced in ISACA's *Risk IT* (**www.isaca.org/riskit**) and can be found directly at **fairwiki.riskmanagementinsight.com**.

Factor analysis adds probabilities (frequencies in a given amount of time [one year] or guesstimates, depending on what is reliably available and has the least bias) to each of the aspects (factors and steps) of the cascade in the scenario. Because these are unfolding events, root-cause (not just proximate-cause) information is needed.

The numerical values are based on sources of information appropriate to each factor:

- External non-institution-specific sources. For example, weather, cyber-terrorism, country risk conditions or economic analysis. This may be more or less quantified.

- External institution-aggregated sources. For example, frauds and client issues. These are generally quantified in loss databases.[13]

- External or internal evaluation of a particular threat scenario (e.g. capability of organized crime to penetrate the bank through employees, capability of social unrest to expand and harm operations, or capability of a malicious party to breach data protections).

- Internal judgment view of external events or analyses. For example, competitive, customer behavior, economic forecasts.

- Internal judgment of internal capabilities. For example, product management strength, risk management strength, internal control strength or information technology strength.

After probabilities are assigned and multiplied through the factors in the event chain, the outcomes can be compared to internal and external loss data.

---

[13] Please see cautions on using external loss data sources in chapter 1.7.

A little math:

The probability of two events occurring in a sequence:

```
P(A and B) = P(A) * P(B|A)
P(A and B) = P(A) * P(B) for independent events
```

The probability of at least one of two events occurring:

```
P(A or B) = P(A) + P(B)-P(A and B)
P(A or B) = P(A) + P(B) Mutually exclusive events
```

The probability of failure grows quickly:

```
.9 x .9 x .9 x .9 x .9 x .9 = .531
```
(for independent events)

Various levels of rigor can be applied when conducting factor analysis:

- depth of detail in the scenario factors (actor, object, action, timing, receiving object, impact and consequence)

- depth of detail of events in the event chain (all events, few events, only the end-loss or most proximate-cause events)

- depth of understanding of an event (roll all aspects up into one probability; 'four-factor' approach that looks just at internal and external environment, threat capability and response capability; or more detailed breakdowns of the environment and capability factors as described in the risk management process cycle throughout this book)

- precision in probability and impact estimates.

At one end of the evaluation spectrum, it is a quick judgment by the experts around the workshop table. At the other end, it is a model refined over time that provides penetrating insights for action. The greater the strength of the analysis, the more value it has for stress-testing parameters and, later, designing responses. These are used as inputs to the capital estimates discussed in chapter 1.8 and the priorities discussed in chapter 2.2.

Basing the detailed levels of analysis on a large number of root-cause events, not just proximate-cause events, means that factor analysis has the potential to produce a more accurate and insightful evaluation of risk to return in the institution. This is similar to a large retailer analyzing a supply chain, a manufacturing plant reducing cost and improving quality, or fans betting at a racetrack on an accumulation of tiny details of information.

Tips:

Use the analysis insights to both understand the consequences of 'bad things', and engage the organization to build consensus on the risks to business objectives and the business case to address them. Talk through the scenarios in detail, engaging people in multiple roles and vantage points. **Invite those who most feel or could feel the pain. The process of having the logic conversation about 'why' and root causes can be powerful in motivating action—let the data do the talking to drive the business case for reducing risk.**

Use the word 'risk' with care to avoid confusion in a scenario workshop. For example, some people talk about 'reputation risk'. What is it really? In the discussion of scenarios, there are differences between actors, objects, actions, receiving objects (also called 'targets' or 'assets'), impacts and consequences. In a scenario-analysis workshop walking through a chain of unfolding events in a scenario, it is clear that damage to reputation is usually a consequence. The exception is when a malicious person (such as a disgruntled customer or employee) expressly seeks to do harm to the reputation. In this case, the brand name is the target or asset being attacked.

Participants with different professional backgrounds also use 'risk' differently. Some will think of risk primarily in terms of high uncertainty, some loss and others variance. The steps of the scenario workshop can bring much clarity to terminology when each of these aspects are included in the life-like scenarios.

Summary

The storyboard approach to scenario analysis to help drive business performance (not just compliance) involves several expansions in thinking. These include:

	FROM:	TO:
Scope	Compliance categories	Business environment and processes
Driver	Regulatory compliance	Improve business performance, including compliance
Data perspective	Retrospective loss analysis	Prospective, threat and opportunity analysis
Data store	Loss database	Plus additional operational data and insights
Depth of analysis	Enough to comply	Enough to save business cost and improve
Review timing	Compliance-schedule driven	Business-change driven
Information use	Reporting oriented	Action oriented
Capital charge focus	Increases	Can also decrease from capability improvements

Table used by permission of ValueBridge Advisors, LLC

Looking ahead

Time-sensitive scenarios with root causes will be used in upcoming steps to watch more precisely for warnings, and then in risk-response steps to prioritize and act on them. Actions include improving enterprise capabilities in the institution (or business line or product), in the environment, and/or reshaping the environment.

With so much use in following steps, the quality of scenarios is critical. Thus, we next turn to evaluating scenario quality.

Key points

- Create life-like scenarios, look up and downstream for cascading events and coincidences.

- Find now what will seem obvious later when a 'bad thing' has happened.

- Engage the team and have fun!

1.6. Evaluating Scenario Quality and Avoiding Bias

"At my first employer, J.P. Morgan & Co., integrity and discretion were primary values. But two additional refrains were constant: 'What could go wrong if we do this?' And, the constant reminder, 'If you know of something that concerns you, you must surface it up the line.'"

— *Karen Osar*

'Are your scenarios realistic?' 'Do they avoid bias?' 'Are they reliable?' These are the questions asked by auditors, board members and examiners. Asking—and answering—them helps institutions improve risk management maturity, stress testing and business performance.

Life-like scenarios: checking their pulse

As the workshop output is reviewed, tools can help evaluate the quality of the scenarios. A tool to help visualize the 'big picture' of scenario analysis maturity is the spider web or radar diagram. This helps spot opportunities for improving the overall scenario-analysis process.

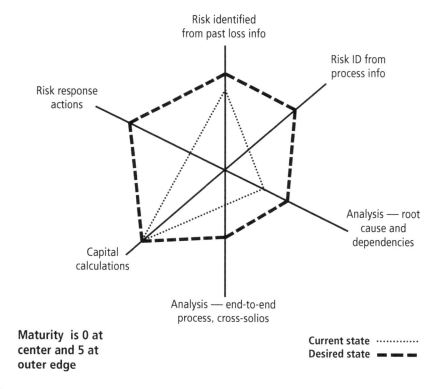

Figure 11

If scenarios are supposed to be life-like, then we can check their pulse. Each storyboard can be 'health checked' against a set of problem criteria:

- Scenarios in organizational silos fail to understand end-to-end business processes and larger activities, including suppliers.

  - They miss root causes and dependencies.

- Scenarios in time silos don't consider the lifecycle view of business activities and processes.

- Scenarios in segments don't consider cascading failures.

- Scenarios created only by specialists don't engage organization-wide insight.

- Scenarios created primarily for compliance purposes (only for capital estimate or control testing) don't tie to performance objectives.

- Too few scenarios make the other limitations worse.

- Did the workshop:
  - Fail to engage key participants from business areas, IT and other improvement teams (BPI, QC, BA, PMO)?
  - Waste time, was boring or even painful?

A key test of quality is the confidence that the so-called 'unknown unknowns' were found. As many public investigations and private post-incident reviews have illustrated, there are few true unknown or mystery causes of incidents. **The question that the public, press and attorneys ask is: 'Who knew what, when?'**

The opportunity for the risk manager is to find out 'who knows *now*' and engage those people in the scenario-analysis workshop and ongoing team.

```
Expected value of better information = Likely profit from
the range of outcomes after research - Likely profit from
the range of outcomes before research.
```

If deeper surveys with a better prototype can lead to a more profitable product, then that is good. However, the amount spent on that research to gain that information must be less than the additional profit potential from making a more informed decision.

The same thought can be applied to risk management. Will the time and effort to seek out and invite two more people to a scenario-analysis workshop (and the time and travel costs of their participation) help turn 'unknowns' into 'knowns?' If so, will the improvement in profitability be greater than the cost of their participation? If so, then it makes sense to bring them into the team now! As a practical matter, given so much concern about unknowns, it is an easy decision to get the right people into the room to help create better scenarios, solutions to the risks identified and improved profitability for the institution.

To be biased is human; to critique is prudent

We all live with our biases. It is very difficult to be the statistical 'unbiased indicator' in real life. Repeated **studies have shown the susceptibility of**

humans to bias in judgment in a wide variety of situations including in gambling, personal health and fitness, motor vehicle driving, purchasing products and in work-life. With so much information already available, just three observations will be made here.

First, the great value of techniques like dependency analysis, scenario analysis, factor analysis and supporting-root-cause techniques is that they push people to structure their judgment in such a way that reduces bias. Indeed, the reason they are so popular with sales executives is that this gets past the optimism of the typical salesperson in forecasting sales results (and it is good that salespeople are optimistic given the rejection they face). In addition to help from the techniques and tools, the **workshop leader can help reduce bias by maintaining a culture where challenge and critique is invited**.

Second, consider the causes of bias. For personal and team reflection (which can be reviewed at the outset and/or conclusion of a workshop) many common causes of bias in institutions can be grouped under the following areas:

Environmental

- Formal authority distortions
- 'no bad news' culture
- conflicts of interest
- participants' perceived expertise
- peer pressure
- fatigue!

Analytical

- Performance pressure
- inexperience in subject matter, evaluation techniques, solution design, response
- current euphoria or failure
- time pressure

- information exposure timing
- externalities.

Psychological

- Group think
- bystander effective/diffusion of responsibility (that is, the tendency of an individual not to act because someone else is perceived as responsible)
- optimism bias
- confirmation bias (that is, the tendency to interpret new information to confirm, rather than challenge, the view we have already formed)
- hypothesis framing
- halo effect
- heuristic/comparison errors (or rigging)
- hindsight or recency bias
- conjunction bias (more detail, less probable)
- anchoring and adjustment
- framing of benefits and risk.

Fight bias until it is common to question unusual situations and 'blind-sides' in decision-making, and play 'devil's advocate'. The unusual situation need not be a reason to stop the risky activity. The point is that risks taken in pursuit of reward are fully understood.

Key points

- Check the 'pulse' of scenarios to confirm they are life-like.
- Engage 'people who know' now in workshops, not after bad things happen.
- Proactively fight each type of bias with the right weapons.

1.7. Creating Insightful Single Sources of Risk Information

"Getting early warning and root-cause information assumes that we have a reasonable number of places to look and can integrate that information. Having a single source of truth makes it easier to find patterns in information and understand what actions are needed, how quickly, and to respond to the situation."

— *Humphrey Polanen*

Information to provide answers

After creating a robust analysis of risks to return, this information must be gathered in one spot that is easily accessible, so as to answer questions such as:

- What is the total risk to performance to which we are exposed across the systems—by a business activity within our institution, by our institution itself or by our institution within a broader system?

- How does a change in the environment ripple through all the risks and scenarios to change the amount of risk we face (for bad or good)?

- How does our understanding of risk scenarios point us to common root causes and responses that can efficiently reduce risk from multiple but related threat types? How does this help us better manage that risk to be more competitive than other companies?

- How does our understanding of our risk point us to more opportunities?

- How does our understanding of risk enable us to better allocate acceptable risk by business line, functional area or geographic region?

To enable more actionable insight from an easily accessible and updatable source, a single source of information should be created and maintained. This source might be referred to as a risk profile or risk catalog. This structure also forms the data structure for the loss database.

Organizing information more efficiently

Ideally, the single source brings together the information from the risk management cycle (risk evaluation and response) plus a project management view (owner, actions, dates, resources, status).

These can be implemented at various levels of detail. There are a variety of helpful software tools (at varying levels of scale and cost) that make this task far more efficient. General software such as spreadsheets and basic databases can help. Special purpose software tools often include content management, workflow, dashboard/reporting capabilities and starting templates. A comprehensive breakdown of capabilities is provided in the Open Compliance and Ethics Group (OCEG) technology blueprint located at **www.oceg.org**. This document benefits from the years of research by the chair of OCEG's technology council, Michael Rasmussen, the leading industry analyst in this space and founder of the firm Corporate Integrity.

The right data organized the right way to make your job easier

Going beyond the basics and product-specific questions, here are particular data elements that can help get more business insight from the data:

- **Business activity link**: Make the connection between a risk and a business activity clear. Whether by sorting through spreadsheet column indicators or advanced business intelligence, be able to create a clear view of risk relevant to a business activity (line, functional area, geographic region). This is key for viewing risk to specific business outcomes, assigning accountability to fix risks and more appropriate operational risk capital allocations.

- **Business performance measure link**: Include an element that ties the risk to specific business performance measures/indicators that are relevant to the executive who owns the risk and is accountable for fixing it.

- **Threat type**: Indicate whether the threat source is malicious, natural, accidental, agency-related or connected with business/transaction volume.

- **Threat source**: Indicate whether the threat originates inside or outside the institution.

- **Event chain step**: As risks are a chain of unfolding events, indicate where in a chain a specific database entry falls among upstream and downstream events. This can be by indicator or by logical groups in the chain of unfolding events. This information comes from the scenario analysis. This can include the number or name of the preceding event in the chain and the following event in the chain. It can be a very simple indicator for smaller or less mature institutions. Plan ahead to design this capability into your database for future use.

- **Ability to detect**: Indicate the capability of an institution to detect that a problem is occurring. Indicate with a simple 1–5 scale. In reports, this will help you identify blind spots.

- **Frequency**: Record the frequency with which the event occurs in a specific time interval.

- **Impact**: State the stage in the unfolding chain at which the event is being recorded in this entry. Include both historical and predictive values.

- **Typical cumulative impact**: Record the impact across all stages of an unfolding chain of events. This entry will be the same for all the individual events that make up the chain.

- **Risk response type**: State what specific action type will be taken to fix a process problem or reduce a risk. This makes it easier to visualize the high-benefit risk-response actions.

- **Risk/threat type knowledge**: Indicate how well the risk type is understood. Not all risks will immediately be part of a solid scenario-analysis workshop. Some will be waiting their turn. Flagging the depth of understanding provides insight for prioritization and status.

- **Risk response knowledge**: Indicate how well the risk response is understood. Again, not all risks will immediately have a clear response plan. Flagging the depth of understanding provides insight for prioritization and status.

- **Gap rating**: Indicate the gap rating from the heat map analysis showing the executive view of how well the risk has been addressed to date compared to how well the risk should be addressed. This will aid in generating consolidated gap-based heat maps from your database. (Please see chapter 2.2 for more about heat maps based on gap analysis.)

- **Risk response decision**: Indicate whether a risk was accepted, transferred/shared, avoided or mitigated/reduced.

- **Risk responses purpose**: Indicate whether a response action is intended to prevent something from happening; prepare for the inevitable; or reduce/slow or stop the chain when the inevitable occurs.

- **Ability to control**: Indicate the ability of your stopping power. If the negative event occurs, what is your ability to slow, reduce or stop it, assuming you are first able to detect it? Indicate on a 1–5 scale.

- **Independent assurance reviews**: Record date and outcome of past reviews.

In all these entries, information is recorded at the available level of detail. This partially depends on the size of an institution, the nature of a scenario, and level of maturity of the institution in risk analysis. More summarized entries tend to depend more on longer narrative descriptions. More detailed entries rely more on short phrases and words and pointers to related information. Regardless of the approach taken, sufficient information on the upstream and downstream events should be included so that a person preparing reports and/or graphs can locate information and then display an unfolding scenario or event flow chain.

Finally, structure any free text entries in a way that always points to a) the business objective at risk and b) the dependencies.

This level of information meets both business performance needs and would seem to meet the needs of Basel. The primary guidance for loss data collection comes from the internal data section (670–674) of the AMA Soundness Standard of *A Revised Framework*. This is enhanced by the instructions for the loss data collection exercises. A key statement is: "A bank's internal loss data must be *comprehensive* in that it captures all material activities and exposures from all appropriate *sub-systems and geographic locations*" (emphasis added).

Use caution in adding external to internal data. To use external data, it must be assumed that loss events are independent and institutions in which the losses occurred are similar in terms of both environment, and design and maturity of their enterprise process capabilities. Both assumptions are weak. This can be easily seen by walking through a chain of cascading events in a scenario-analysis workshop or observing capability differences across institutions. Use of external loss data also assumes all losses are reported at the same thresholds and with similar root-cause detail. Other cautions also apply. A helpful discussion is found in section 8.7 of *A New Approach for Managing Operational Risk*, (Society of Actuaries, revised, 2010).

With the results of your risk evaluation brought together in an accessible, living way, the next steps are to use the data for capital estimates and to inform the design of risk indicators.

Key points

- The objective of a single source of risk information is to make it easier to get good answers.

- General and specific-purpose software can make this task more efficient.

- Within whatever tool is used, it is crucial to organize information in a way that makes it easier to understand how risks unfold in chains within a system.

1.8. Capital Estimates: Trips, Traps and Pitfalls

"Basel requires banks to cover various types of operational risk exposures with allocated capital. Whether or not you believe that increased capital is a way of safeguarding against higher risk, we are in an era where the calibration and management of operational risk will be increasingly important for banks. There will be clear penalties for banks that don't do it well."

— *Ron Dietz*

Capital estimates and loss data—don't miss the forest

From a regulatory perspective, the 'fundamental objective' of the Basel Committee has been to "strengthen the soundness and stability of the international banking system while maintaining sufficient consistency that capital adequacy regulation will not be a significant source of competitive inequality among internationally active banks". [14]

'Soundness and stability' is achieved through holding capital at a level reflecting the risk taken by an institution, including operational risks.

From a regulatory perspective, this begins with loss data collection (LDC).

---

[14] *A Revised Framework*, paragraph 4.

Basel II, *A Revised Framework*, section 665 and following refers to "four fundamental" data elements: internal loss data, external data, scenario analysis, and business environment and internal control factors (BEICFs) for use with the operational risk advanced measurement approach (AMA).

Loss event types for Basel reporting are:

- internal fraud

- external fraud

- employment practices and workplace safety

- clients, products and business practices

- damage to physical assets

- business disruption and system failures

- execution, delivery and process management.

From both a business performance and regulatory perspective, the purpose of holding operational risk capital is to *provide capacity to absorb loss that might arise from risk in pursuit of return.* This is perfectly natural in all aspects of life; for example, our personal preferences when it comes to buying extended warranties on consumer goods, making decisions on deductibles on insurance policies or being willing to play high-risk sports.

In balancing risk with capacity to absorb loss, we consider the impact—'How bad could it be?' When considering the magnitude of loss, we consider the impact of controls and preparedness to help detect, slow, contain or stop loss in an unfolding chain of events. Techniques for reducing loss will be discussed in the chapters on responding to risk. For now, the point is that the ability to absorb loss (capital cushion) is balanced against likelihood and impact given actions for controls and preparedness *against root or intermediate causes of risk.*

Approaches to capital modeling and trouble with techniques

When a particular airplane has a serious in-flight problem, the news reports may initially state that all similar planes are grounded. As more information comes out, this will be refined to planes of a similar age or with similar parts, such as a specific engine or instrument. With further information on the cause, mechanics might be told to look for similar use situations or warning signs. In other words, to protect the flying public and still serve passengers getting from one place to another, the focus narrows with information pertaining to the root cause. No one would say: 'Don't bother, keep flying, just add more capital to pay claims.' But that's effectively how it is with models for estimating operational risk capital.

The trouble is that modeling techniques used in the past few years have had difficulty reflecting systems and root causes in risk to operations for financial companies. For example, most financial institutions have tried to adapt credit and market techniques. However, the lack of data and fundamental differences of risk to operations make this approach questionable. Without getting into math, at least six limitations are evident:

- Insufficient number of data points. In particular, lack of the root-cause data necessary to make causal predictions.

- Lack of clarity on loss. Models often capture a loss at only one point in the chain of unfolding events—often one that exceeds a threshold for that one stage. This misses the upstream and downstream losses in the chain in a system. While this missed data would raise capital estimates, it could also be used in business case benefits from fixing the source of the risk. Worse, contagions can spread widely before they cross a threshold and are noticed.

- Lack of understanding about how things work. Without realistic scenario analysis of how events unfold and cascade, it is difficult (if not impossible) to reflect the full potential losses or the benefits of fixing them. Importantly, just adding root cause data points (and hopefully they are root causes) is different from actually modeling a system where root cause triggers a row of dominos to fall.

- Models that assume independence fly in the face of what we have learned about systems theory and the interconnectedness of events. This gets worse when attempts are made to aggregate risks in categories that are interdependent—as in the case of Basel categories that are not mutually exclusive.

- Value at Risk (VaR) as a matter of definition does not capture risk beyond a selected confidence level (e.g. 95%).

- Failure to acknowledge limits. The above and other limitations reduce confidence levels and raise a range of interpretive problems.

Capital estimate—overcoming barriers to getting value from VaR

Contributed by: Deborah Cernauskas, Gabriel David, Anthony Tarantino [15]

How managers deal with operational risk depends on which camp they ascribe to: those advocating VaR and those advocating a qualitative, judgmental approach to decision-making. The quants are searching for the best-fitting distribution to facilitate their VaR calculations. The qualitative camp argues that the quant models have failed and it is time to go back to basics. We believe both approaches are misguided.

Many risk managers have chosen to use a VaR model to measure their capital requirements. This is due to operational risk exposure under the advanced measurement approach of Basel. Quantitative risk managers are at ease with VaR as it has been used as a measure of portfolio risk since the early 1990s.

VaR's ease of use and accessibility helped spur its adoption, despite its mathematical deficiencies being known for many years. Many quants have convinced themselves that VaR limitations can be overcome by finding a better-fitting distribution and adding a little scenario analysis for long-tail testing (not to be confused with the more robust scenario analysis described elsewhere in this book).

For too many years, financial researchers have been modeling risks under the assumption that losses follow some underlying distribution and the challenge is to find the correct distribution or mixture of distributions. Unfortunately, the multidimensional nature of the risk of a complex system (e.g. the operations of a bank) cannot be adequately modeled by a single distribution or mixture of distributions, nor can it be through the use of discrete event simulation embodied in scenario analysis.

As an alternative, *qualitative* risk management is based on managers following a rational decision-making process. Bazerman (1998) outlined a six-step form of this that entails:

[15] Deborah Cernauskas, PhD, Risk and Technology Corp., Northern Illinois University, DeKalb, IL; Gabriel David, senior risk management advisor; Anthony Tarantino, PhD Santa Clara University, Santa Clara, CA.

1. fully defining the problem

2. identifying all criteria

3. accurately weighing the criteria according to significance

4. identifying all alternatives

5. assessing each alternative according to the criteria

6. choosing the best alternative.[16]

Rational decision-making involves following these six steps. But human beings are not rational creatures. Herbert Simon's Nobel-Prize-winning research proposed that humans use bounded rationality in decision-making but human rationality is constrained by several factors including: limited information; time and cost constraints; limited ability to synthesize complex situations; and judgment biases based on experience.[17] Additionally, research has illustrated the systematic biases that influence judgment and decision-making. Overwhelming research suggests the need to avoid bias and the difficulty in doing so.

What's the answer?

We suggest a research-based line of reasoning: namely, that the current focus of quantitative risk managers to find the optimal loss distribution is misguided because of the nature of operational risk, especially that the inclusion of external data hurts both the model quality and the effort to actually fix root causes of risk. Furthermore, we propose a modified approach to VaR that spotlights risk factors and the use of agent-based modeling and simulation (ABMS) to capture the bounded rationality of human decision-making.

---

[16] Bazerman, Max. (1998) *Judgment in Managerial Decision Making.* (Hoboken, New Jersey: John Wiley and Sons).

[17] Simon, Herbert A. (1986) 'Rationality in Psychology & Economics', *The Journal of Business*, Vol. 59, No. 4, Part 2.

Operational risk: modeling a system

A business can be characterized as a combination of processes that enable business functions. For example, the business functions of a bank include extending loans to individuals and businesses. The processes used to enable this example business function include:

- loan application and approval

- deposit taking and management

- wealth management

- foreign exchange trading

- global custody

- cash management

- capital management

- compliance

- information technology management

- trade processing

- payments processing.

People and computer systems are the two fundamental enablers of any business process. A process can fail and lead to an operational loss due to a diverse array of problems, including but not limited to employees not following prescribed governance procedures; software problems; spreadsheet errors; and inadequately trained employees.

Basel defines operational risk as "the risk of loss resulting from inadequate or failed internal processes, people and systems or from external events." This definition can sometimes be misleading. It should not be interpreted to mean that processes, people and systems are elements that operate independently. Rather, people and systems are interconnected and are the fundamental building blocks of a business process capability that can be impacted by external environmental events. With the Basel definition and clarification of it in mind, we can more easily see that operational risk and market risk differ significantly. Operational risk lives in a physical world of processes dependent on people and systems. The data points of interest are root causes that trigger cascades of unfolding events. By sharp contrast, market risk lives in a more mathematic world of price and volume data points (especially for technical traders).

VaR was originally developed as a measure of market risk and then adopted as a measure of operational risk and capital requirements. Given the difference in operational risk, successfully measuring operational risk requires moving away from standard implementations of VaR to include the drivers of risk in physical systems. This includes factors such as process simplicity and organization governance. External factors that drive market risk have a similar affect on firms with similar trading positions. By contrast, in operational risk, using a mix of external and internal factors would reflect a wider range of firm-specific business process and governance structure effects.

The loss distribution approach (LDA) to measuring operational risk under Basel requires combining internal and external data to arrive at a more accurate estimate of the tail of the loss distribution.

The issues involved in combining internal and external data for operational risk modeling has been the focus of other studies. Public sources of loss data have been available for several years from companies such as Fitch and loss-data consortiums such as the Operational Riskdata eXchange (ORX) and the British Bankers Association (BBA). There is general agreement in the industry of the presence of a size bias in publicly collected loss data. Alternatively, loss data available from consortiums also present modeling problems.

Research on the accuracy of parameter estimation when utilizing external data and a variable threshold was the focus of a 2002 study by Baud, Frachot, and Roncalli.[18] Their study assumed the same underlying distribution generated both internal and external data. This is a crucial assumption. The study found that the pooling of internal and external data leads to higher capital charges because of the variable thresholds used. We contend that capital modeling that relies on combining internal and external data has the tendency to create a more skewed distribution, raising the capital level for all the banks in the sample.[19] The combined data cannot be blended together

---

[18] Baud, Nicholas, Frachot, Antoine, and Roncalli, Thierry. (2002), 'Internal date, external data and consortium data for operational risk measurement: How to pool data properly?'. Operational Risk Group, Credit Lyonnais white paper.

[19] Cernauskas, Deborah, David, Gabriel, and Tarantino, Anthony. (2010), 'VaR, VaR, Voom', (**bit.ly/kcTrd7**).

without extensive knowledge of the processes underlying the external data. In other words, it was a bit like analyzing the reasons for differences in pepperoni the placement of pizzas, even though the pizzas compared came from multiple pizza restaurants, prepared by different cooks, each using different instruction guides—without any knowledge of those underlying differences. This is vastly different from the owner of one pizza restaurant with a single instruction guide analyzing variations by cook. This is a structural stumbling block to the aspiration of Basel that the capital model should create incentives for better risk management. A capital-based incentive for process improvement simply cannot exist when external data are required for capital determination.

VaR plus agent-based modeling

Operational losses are the result of failed processes, systems, and human error. VaR focuses on realized losses (i.e. it is outcome based) and does not take into account the underlying risk drivers. Other variations of VaR, including conditional VaR (CVaR) and the extreme value theorem (EVT) approach do not address this important issue.[20] The multidimensional nature of the risk within a financial institution—with all the interdependencies and root causes in the system—renders an outcome-based approach such as VaR structurally inadequate as a risk management or measurement technique.

VaR can be improved through the inclusion of an agent-based modeling and simulation (ABMS) component—both the base model and stress testing. ABMS has been used for many years within social and life sciences and is quickly moving into mainstream finance in areas such as trader behavior. ABMS can model business processes by using independent and interrelated agents (e.g. computer software or employees). Defining and modeling an agent's behavior is an essential component of the overall agent-based model. The behavior models can range from simplistic heuristics to complex artificial intelligence (AI) models. Sophisticated ABMS applications contain agents that learn from their experiences.

---

[20] Mignola and Ugoccioni describe an analysis performed in a controlled environment where they attempted to estimate using EVT the parameters of a known distribution. They compared the simulation results for the expected loss (EL) and the capital at risk (CAR) at the 99.9th quantile to the true distribution values. They found that EL and CAR were not accurately estimated even for large datasets. See: North, Michael and Macal, Charles. (2007), 'Agent-Based Modeling and Simulation: Desktop ABMS'. Proceedings of the 2007 Winter Simulation Conference, 95–106. And: Mignola, Giulio and Ugoccioni, Roberto. (2006), 'Tests of Extreme Value Theory Applied to Operational Risk Data', *The Advanced Measurement Approach to Operational Risk*, ed. Ellen Davies, (London: Risk Books).

Conclusion

Operational risk is multidimensional and complex, thus dictating a new approach to risk management. The current outcome-based approach to VaR is structurally inadequate. VaR as currently applied relies on handpicked scenario generation to identify extreme losses. In complex and interrelated financial networks, it is difficult to identify the exact combination of factors that will lead to extreme losses. ABMS is a bottom-up modeling technique that overcomes this limitation by focusing on risk drivers, eliminating the need for external data. ABMS will allow capital requirements to be uniquely determined by the state of a business' own processes (employees, systems, etc.) and environment in which they operate. The expenditures for process improvements will be reflected in their capital requirements, thus incentivizing financial institutions to review, upgrade and improve their processes.

Key points

- Capital (in financial institutions) is held to absorb loss that might arise from risk.

- Commonly used loss-distribution modeling techniques have several structural limitations.

- Agent-based modeling and simulation contains approaches that overcome the limitations of other methods.

1.9. Capital and Performance Incentives

Moving loss data analysis from a compliance to a performance basis

"I don't want to be the 'angel of death,'" said one risk manager. "I don't want business leaders to only see me as 'bad news.'"

To more easily make the shift from a compliance-oriented to a business-performance-oriented risk management approach, three enhancements to your institution's loss database are helpful. These are *not* required for compliance purposes. They are used for more fully understanding the performance impact.

First, capture losses on the entire chain of events. To make this easier, each step in the unfolding event chain can carry an identifier such as xxxx.xxxx.nnnn.xxxx.xxxx where the left most numbers are the proximate cause and the right most numbers for the root cause. There can be as many number groups as necessary to capture the event chain. In *A Revised Framework*, section 669 (c) states: "A bank's risk measurement system must be sufficiently 'granular' to capture the major drivers of operational risk affecting the shape of the tail of the loss estimates." Section 673 includes a clause briefly referencing causes "...as well as some descriptive information about the drivers or causes of the loss event..." From a performance perspective, to reduce risk, cut cost or improve efficiency—it's all about knowing the business.

Second, add opportunity costs. These include the inability to take advantage of business opportunities and loss of revenue because of difficulties in M&A,

new products or geographic expansion plans (e.g. IT was not ready to support a new product launch). In the scenario-analysis workshop, these numbers often easily come from missed revenue forecasts.[21]

Third, add losses that result from daily errors and waste. These are high-frequency events with low individual loss amounts resulting from daily errors and wastes. These often fall under the *de minimis* threshold of many financial institutions. In the 2008 loss data collection exercise (LDCE) only 44 of 119 institutions had a threshold of less than 1000 euros.[22] Of those, anecdotal evidence suggests that many banks don't pick up production losses simply because they fall outside a compliance perception of loss. Yet a little number multiplied by a big number is a big number in risk to performance and big potential savings. Those savings strengthen business cases for actions to reduce risk to the business. A convenient source of information on such losses may come from your quality improvement, business process improvement, business analysis, product management or business operations teams—just look for the people who experience the daily pain of such inefficiency the most. Invite them to your team to share their perspective and join in the party.

Together, moving to a performance perspective based on how the business works (i.e. systems with dependencies and cascading events) **builds rigor into the quantitative model to avoid errors** (e.g. plane crashes based on the frequency of root causes, rather than just the number of plane crashes).

Reducing capital by reducing risk

As noted earlier, the Basel committee seeks to have institutions create incentives to dynamically manage and reduce risk. Further, the Basel Committee expresses the hope that the business environment and internal control factor evaluation will be more forward-looking to reflect improvements in business capabilities. Yet several features of Basel, such as proximate-cause-based modeling with significant smoothing of distributions, work against those aspirations.

---

[21] "Opportunity costs/lost revenues" are referenced as items "important for risk management although they may be beyond the scope required for quantification", in the BCBS 'Operational Risk—Supervisory Guidelines for the Advanced Measurement Approaches' consultative document (paragraph 89c).

[22] Table ILD1, 'Results from the 2008 Loss Data Collection Exercise for Operational Risk', July 2009, BCBS Publication 160a.

The good news is that the root-cause-based systems approach provides a) more forward-looking immediacy and reliability (reducing prediction error) due to increased data points (root-cause data points being more numerous than proximate-cause data points) and b) event flows to add realism and meaning. Using the tools and techniques described earlier, more accurate information can be made in enterprise capabilities—oversight, management, controls, and core business products and processes. When the improvements are to the quality of the risk governance and management process itself, they can be reflected in the so-called 'Pillar 2' adjustment (the second pillar of the revised framework being the supervisory review process, discussed in part 3 of the framework).

This provides the opportunity for financial institutions to more directly receive the benefits of reduced capital due to reduced risk from improved enterprise capability. This would put financial institutions in the same category as enterprises in other industries who balance capital and risk. For example, in manufacturing, distribution and repair services, the portion of working capital used to fund inventory safety stock levels is reduced *directly* by reducing risk and improving efficiency and risk management in inventory management.

To be sure, capital will increase as external threats increase or internal capabilities decrease. The key is that improvements in capability are reflected in reductions to required capital.

Allocating capital to functional areas

Allocating operational risk capital to functional areas can be a painful exercise. No executive wants extra capital darkening the functional area books. Yet when the business performance approach is taken to operational risk, the functional allocation becomes straightforward because the dependency analysis made clear how financial products depend on business processes that in turn depend on support from a variety of functional areas such as marketing or information technology.

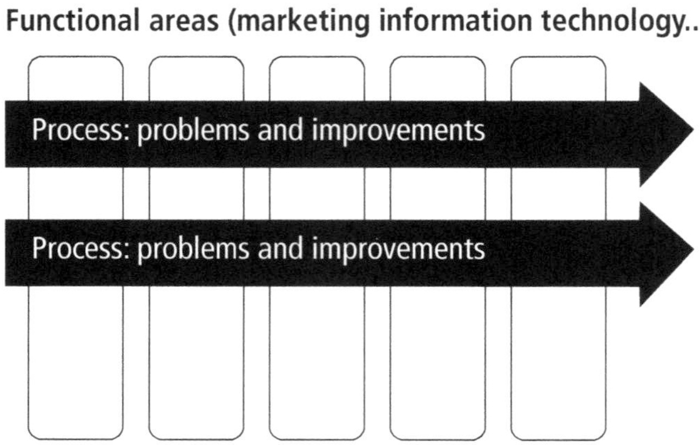

Functional areas (marketing information technology...)

Figure 12

In this way, the internal allocation debate is reduced because 'the number' falls out of a matrix driven by process flow and root cause under that process flow. Root cause is assigned to functional owners.

> **Tip**: There may be some cause-effect debates among functional owners (especially around people versus automation causes), but that is healthy. It leads to solutions. Each relevant functional owner benefits from the fix. And the direct link makes the benefit more transparent and immediate. The clear credit for fixes also serves as justification for improving business cases and separates efficiency issues from business policy questions. It aids the budget process for improvements.

Key points

- To shift loss data analysis from a compliance to performance basis, adjustments are made to capture the entire chain of events and opportunity losses.

- Approaches to capital modeling that use root-cause-based systems make the reduction in capital a more direct result of capability improvements.

- Dependency analysis used in scenario analysis can also be used to more clearly allocate capital to functional areas.

1.10. Watch for Warnings

Risk to operations management cycle

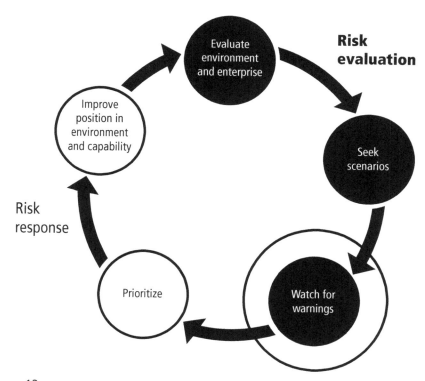

Figure 13

"The biggest problem I see is the lack of support systems to understand the early warnings of the condition of the institution. We need information that is timely enough to enable us to act to avoid problems and take advantage of opportunities. Periodic reports don't fix problems; they don't provide performance to shareholders."

— *Humphrey Polanen*

Watching the right things to reduce risk to objectives

Our focus is on achieving business performance objectives. We want to reduce the risk to outcomes. To this point in part 1 we have evaluated the 'what' (environment and enterprise capabilities) and the 'how' (scenarios unfolding in time).

At this point, a workshop participant will likely ask: 'There are so many moving parts, what exactly should I watch?' To focus our watchful eye, we use the prior steps of the risk management cycle.

What to watch: environment, capability, outcomes

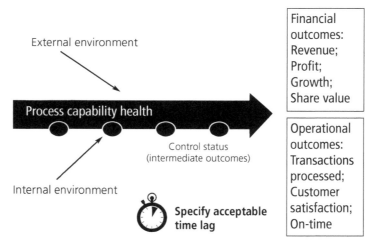

Figure 14

Environment

This includes challenges and opportunities outside and inside the enterprise that increase or decrease the institution's risk to return.

Capability

This is the health of business product processes from idea to delivery. Business process is the big defender because strength here can be used to repel threats and, better take advantage of environmental change to seize opportunities for profitable growth.

Outcomes

Financial outcomes include key metrics such as revenue, expense, assets, liabilities, capital categories and cash flow (liquidity). Operational outcomes include market share growth, efficiency/productivity, on-time performance and customer satisfaction.

Intermediate measures

These include information provided by control points in business processes. These usually are operational in nature (errors, exceptions, rework and other flags).

Timing

The key question is acceptable lag time for reporting a given measure—quarter, month, week, day, hour, minute or second — in view of potential loss or opportunity missed.

Risk range

These indicators provide a view of the range of threats to the range of business operations embraced in scenario analysis. This includes the following:

- The full range of operational threat types (malicious, natural, accidental, business volume/transaction levels and agency). Including this breadth is sometimes referred to as an 'all-threats' or 'all-hazards' view.

- The range of business activities (business lines, products, functional, geographic).

- The range of business assets (people, intellectual property, information technology [applications, middleware, data storage, services, networking, IT process management software]), other business property and facilities.

Ability to detect

In evaluating capabilities, a key need is the ability to detect looming problems and see in dark corners. Ability to detect is so important that in some industries (such as hospitals and electric utilities) it is a classification factor.

Problems can be *external* events, such as detecting a tsunami and providing early warning. Or, they can be *internal* processes that can be more closely monitored or measured with controls. For now, key considerations are: the ability to detect to any extent; the ability to detect accurately (without false signals); and the time lag from the problem occurring to detection.

Regarding extent of insight, consider your own car. What is on the dashboard? Detailed gauges to tell you what is wrong (like an airplane cockpit) or a single 'check engine' light that can mean anything from a serious problem to a reminder to stop in at the dealer every 5000 miles—or something in between. Warning lights can provide varying levels of actionable information.

Regarding timing, what is crucial is how early the warning is given and how closely that warning points to root cause. Can you detect the first tremor of the earthquake? The first cyber-intrusion attempt? The first high-risk trade by an employee desperate to recover from a prior trading loss? Detecting too late lets a chain of events unfold further and cause more damage.

Finally, the ability to detect early is important for more than the mechanical benefit of preventing, slowing or stopping an unfolding chain of events. The ability to detect also has information implications. If someone else knows and you don't know, that gives a competitor or a malicious party the ability to exploit that knowledge against you. This is called asymmetric information. For example, mobile banking and electronic cash transfer services are both growing quickly. This combination can enable money laundering on a large scale. Or in trading, many managers (line and risk) have difficulty seeing or calculating the true risk of products in which traders have positions. Thus they set incorrect limits. Traders seeking profit then exploit these limit errors. The rest is history.

In summary, having the ability to *detect* is a prerequisite to *managing*. In trading, the ability to immediately see changes is crucial. In some disciplines, detection ability is so important that the capability is tracked as a key indicator of management process health. If you are flying blind in an airplane, the likelihood of safely reaching home is low.

Key risk indicators (KRIs) provide some value by simply existing. When bias was discussed earlier, it was noted that humans suffer from perception problems. One is being able to know that something is bad while inside that situation. By predefining boundaries of warning—before being in the situation—we can guard against that bias and respond to the warnings.

KRIs operate at several levels. These levels can be confused. Top-level risk indicators are directly tied to key performance indicators, such as performance indicators used in executive compensation. For example, the risk of error in trade settlement. They can also be tied to financial measures such as net income. On the next level are the more significant causal factors that drive the KRIs. For example, a failure of two IT systems to properly match data. Below this are indicators looking at other causal factors. Indicators can provide a view of different points of an unfolding chain of events. Some indicators are intended to be leading (as in leading indicators of economic downturn) or concurrent (as in a stock trade monitor). The types of lower level indicators, especially those looking at causes that are leading indicators, should be expected to change over time with changes in the environment and enterprise capabilities.

To understand more about the ability to detect, we move to how to watch.

A sharp lookout—how to watch

To watch each type of measurement, the right tool is needed.

To provide more insight for action, it is helpful to distinguish between reporting on the environmental situation and enterprise capability.

- Situation reporting asks: 'What is the likelihood trading volume in this session will exceed our computing capacity to support it?'

- Capability reporting asks: 'What is our strength in a given area (e.g. IT or product management) in terms of skilled people, processes and tools to provide the level of service needed to reduce the risk of failure?'

Both of these types of reporting are about the risk to which the institution is exposed right now—after earlier risk response actions were taken (sometimes this is termed 'residual risk'). That said, the reports differ on time-sensitivity and options to respond. It's a bit like a small boat in a storm—the situational risk is about the waves that could swamp the boat. This is immediate. The capability risk is about the design of the boat to resist capsizing, and preparations with abandon-ship gear if the boat does capsize. In the storm, there is little the skipper can do about capability factors. The point of providing insights on capabilities is to drive actions that strengthen capabilities and thus options (and associated costs) to respond to the risk expressed in the situational analysis.

Caution: Residual risk is sometimes treated as a rather static concept to be visited infrequently. This can give a false sense of comfort. *Residual risk is something for constant re-evaluation.* Depending on the scenario of threats and capabilities, the residual risk can change on a weekly, daily, hourly or more frequent basis.

To simplify analysis of these different types of measures, one of two types of tools can be used:

Watch for warnings with the right tools

Environment and events	Enterprise capability
Pattern analysis using: • Root-cause data • Event flows	Benchmark maturity for: • Gaps • Improvements

Figure 15

Environment and events

The primary tool for seeing warning signs in the environment and unfolding events (external or internal) is pattern analysis. To generate insights, pattern analysis draws on root-cause data and event flows.

Data sources and risk indicators

In the external environment, both external data sources (weather, terror, crime and more) and internal sensors of external events (like cyber-intrusion detection) provide data (the closer to the source or root cause the better).

For internal events, controls generate data on variation from control limits (or tolerance).

Risk indicators draw on controls and environmental data sources to indicate whether performance might fall outside of defined acceptable tolerance from business objectives (performance). A tolerance is some range (such as +/- 5%, around an objective (such as a stock price). Some tolerances are two-way, while others are one-way. Some indicators are directly based on an external measure over which an institution has no control (such as a rise in cyber threats). Others are based on an internal process that an institution can control (such as knowing your customer controls, or coping with snow or rain tracked onto the marble floor of your lobby).

KRIs can have a variety of attributes. Among open standards, frameworks and guidance, ISACA's *Risk IT* (**www.isaca.org/riskit**) probably spends the most time on KRIs. *Risk IT* recommends several criteria for selecting KRIs:

- impact—indicators for risks with high business impact are more likely to be KRIs

- effort to implement, measure and report—for different indicators that are equivalent in sensitivity, the one that is easier to measure is preferred

- reliability—the indicator must possess a high correlation with the risk and be a good predictor or outcome measure

- sensitivity—the indicator must be representative for risk and capable of accurately indicating variances in the risk.

These KRI criteria help select indicators that actually flag when root causes are in motion and hopefully also point to the needed corrective action. Timely and good data makes pretty pictures. To provide business benefit, pretty pictures must become *insight for action*—situational awareness. This requires adding an understanding of how events unfold.

Event flows

Event flows provide an understanding of how events unfold from root causes to impacts and consequences. This is the understanding that was built earlier in the chapter on scenario analysis. Combining event flows with the root-cause data (including KRIs) makes pattern analysis possible.

Pattern analysis

Understanding how events unfold from the root-cause events that are flagged as early warnings enables an institution to take action. This is exactly what a trader with technical analysis software does when comparing data points to trading ranges (control limits or risk tolerances) and then applies understanding of how events might unfold in order to make a trading decision. Pattern analysis not only improves awareness of potential danger and missed opportunity, but also helps avoid wasting resources on the wrong issues.

If based on root-cause, *leading* indicators give what military analysts call 'predictive battlespace awareness'. Whether Sun Tzu used that phrase or not, in your financial institution this could keep you solvent, ahead of competitors and/or help you crisply implement a new product or market.

The defense: enterprise capability

Enterprise capabilities provide the defense to incoming threats, whether from external or internal sources. Capabilities are also crucial because they enable an organization to bring together people, tools and plans to achieve business objectives.

These capabilities can be grouped: governance; management; controls; and core business product cycle (analyze, develop, market, sell, deliver, support).

Risk governance will be addressed later. The core business product cycle is also briefly addressed later in the chapter on using the product management process to better manage risk.

Here, we'll focus on evaluating the capability of the risk management function and processes. Risk management capability includes quality of processes, skills (including training and certifications) and outcomes (efficiency and effectiveness in reaching business outcome objectives).

A now-classic approach to evaluating management capability is through benchmarking capabilities using maturity models. Capability maturity models (CMMs) were popularized by Carnegie Mellon University's Software Engineering Institute (SEI), initially for the purpose of improving the quality of software development and systems engineering projects. This measurement approach has since been adapted for many other capability types. For the purposes of operational risk management in financial institutions, the closest models in open use are those found in CMU's Computer Emergency Response Team (CERT)'s resilience management model (**www.cert.org/resilience**) and ISACA's *Risk IT* (**www.isaca.org/riskit**). Another evaluation approach is to use agreed-upon procedures (AUPs) that are procedures for a limited-purpose audit. These are used by OCEG's 'Burgundy Book' (**www.oceg.org**) to evaluate capabilities.

The maturity tables in the SEI and ISACA documents describe a rating scale 0–5 (where 5 is best). An organization determines what description most clearly describes the organization's current state in any capability, and then its desired state for those capabilities. For example, in one area an organization might be a '1' currently, and the management team and board desires the organization to become a '3' in 12 months. In this case, the 'maturity gap' would be 3 minus 1 which equals 2.

In *Risk IT*, each management process is evaluated against five criteria:

- awareness and communication

- responsibility and accountability

- goal setting and measurement

- policies, standards and procedures

- skills and expertise.

Capability maturity assessment can be valuable right out of the box. It can also be tailored to your organization. In addition, these models can be extended to make them more powerful as diagnostics to point to opportunities for improvement. For example, a common difficulty is determining whether a problem is greater in implementation or operations. Other times, it is helpful to make a distinction in whether the pain (and gap) is in organization enablement, process and tools, or training and communications. The faster gaps can be pinpointed, the faster they can be fixed to provide business benefit. To help in such situations, pain-spotting charts are helpful. These are best used in workshops where multiple viewpoints can be collected and used along with other root-cause tools. Just plot the pains in the rows and columns to see the patterns.

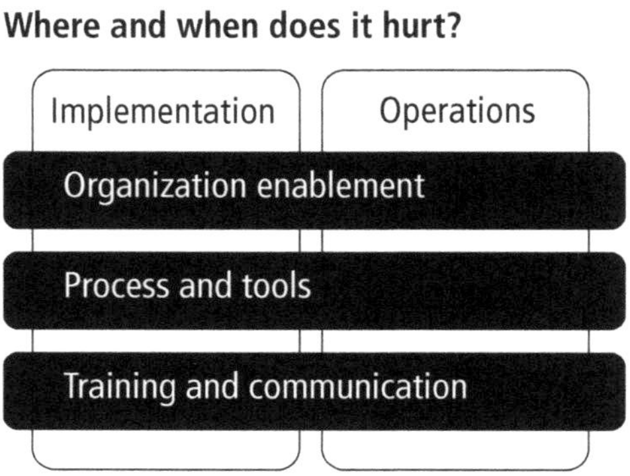

Where and when does it hurt?

Figure 16

Tracking capability improvement on a monthly, quarterly and annual basis can be used by the board of directors, senior management, auditors, and examiners in evaluating the performance of the senior operational risk executive. Conversely, the operational executives can use such evaluations to spot weaknesses in the team, create training plans and budgets, assign improvement objectives to people, and plan hiring.

To make it clear to the board and senior management how capability improvements drive business outcomes, this information can be reported in a three-layer ('birthday cake') scorecard.

The top category is business objectives and the risk to those business objectives. The second layer contains risk management function objectives to support those business objectives. The third layer is progress on strengthening the capabilities of the risk management function.

By starting with familiar business objectives and measurements, risk reporting gains relevance for the board members and senior executives (especially in a matrix of business line, functional and geographic executives).

In addition to the good guidance from these sources, a few points of emphasis are helpful, especially for institutions seeking to place more emphasis on risk management to improve business performance.

For evaluating risk culture, ask:

- Are people *aware of the range of potential threats* to the business and actively scanning for them?

- Are people *building risk-awareness into their decision-making* in a meaningful way? Some industries open all meetings with a 'safety moment'. Are meaningful risk templates built into all decision documents? Are statements of risk actively debated?

- Are people *aware of what information to share* with others and the need to share (past studies have found people communicate more completely and timely when they understand the value of the information)?

- Do people *believe policies* that say anyone can raise the alarm? Are they fearful that they will suffer harm for pointing out problems?

- Do people know *how to respond* when the alarm rings? Do they report that they know their role and what to do? If they are unsure or apprehensive they are likely to delay taking action.

- Do people perceive risk-related *education as personally relevant*? Organizations with large numbers of frontline employees (such as the hospitality industry) have found this is key to making people more aware of identified risks, new risks arising and acting on warning signals.

In short, **culture must have concrete expectations**. From an evaluation perspective, gaps in process can more easily be overcome by strong risk culture, than weaknesses in culture can be by strong process.

For reporting on the 'watching' infrastructure, include: the ability to detect; quality of controls (both design and operations); quality of external environment data sources; and quality of indicators (use the criteria above). In the 2003 North American electric power blackout, a key contributing factor was that monitoring systems were not operating properly at the time of the incident.

For reporting on communication, use a communication map to illustrate whether the right people are getting the right information at the right time. A communication map looks a little like an organization chart, except the roles are coded with symbols that represent RACI roles. The lines connecting roles are color-coded to reflect types of communication. Lines have dashed or solid patterns to indicate leading, concurrent or lagging information. Width of lines can illustrate volume of information – how 'in the loop' a role is. This is an excellent chart to use in cross-unit risk workshops to verify that people are sufficiently engaged. For 'informed' roles, the fix can be as simple as adding a person to an email distribution list. For 'decision' roles, it engages the organization in questions like ownership, true accountability and agility in decision-making.

For reporting on culture, consider policy compared to action. Some organizations have an official policy that anyone can report risk or stop activity. Yet the unofficial pressures and cultures strongly discourage such action. Bad culture can trump good process. Search for the warning signs of problem culture.

Bias can be evaluated with the criteria noted earlier. Here, it is applied to reporting on the warning information. What will be the space shuttle launch decision regarding the o-rings when expressing different engineering assessments is complicated by culture?

In summary, a simplified risk reporting health check can be helpful in providing more clarity and *insight for action*:

- Is it relevant—addresses important concerns and impacts to the business?

    Who (what RACI roles) values the information?

    Why is it valued?

    To what performance (revenue, cost, and customer satisfaction) and compliance objectives does it align? Is this clearly recognized by users?

- Is it actionable? Does it clearly help prevent problems?

    Is the information timely and sufficient to illustrate patterns and identify meaningful root causes?

    Does it cross silos, follow business processes and reflect IT dependencies?

    Does it pass the '5 Whys' test?

    Do leaders see it as enabling more risk-aware decision-making and leading to better outcomes?

- Is it relatively easy?

    Does the source data have sufficient quality (detail and accuracy) and availability?

    Does it have good cost/benefit (for both the risk team and enterprise business team)?

Key points

- Focus needs to be on risk to achieving business objectives (in financial or operational terms).

- Care is needed to create meaningful early warning indicators at several levels.

- Warnings are reported on both an environment situation and capability basis; use the right tool for each analysis.

1.11. Key Insights for Evaluating Risk

In summary, key practical insights from the chapters on evaluating risk are:

- **Take a systems view of risk**—the environment and enterprise capabilities. **Scenarios are your central tool for understanding situations in time**.

- Take a prospective, not retrospective, view of risk evaluation.

- Understand the environment better than competitors. This is a requirement in strategy and operations. It's also a requirement in managing risk to your strategy and operations.

- Understand the business. A deep understanding of how it works is essential to finding and fixing risks before they cause damage, and to using your capabilities to take advantage of opportunities in a changing environment.

- Look for change. Change brings threats and opportunity.

- Find the person who already knows—few risks are truly new in the world.

- Identify the right performance measures and data.

- Select the right tool (approaches, methods, techniques) for the job. Maturing organizations need more efficient tools to be effective more easily.

- **Relentlessly ask 'What if?' 'When?' and 'How long?'** Bring together an understanding of the environment and how the business works through robust scenarios to understand how to seize opportunities and guard against loss.

- Be honest. Rigorously check for bias. Markets, shareholders, competitors, customers and regulators will find them if you don't. Understand causes and types of bias and root them out before they hurt the business and make you look foolish.

- Be vigilant. Watch for warning signs in the environment, capability weakness and outcomes. Minimize lag time and static to create meaningful early warning indicators.

- Drive risk evaluation to improve business performance. Focusing on real performance should also cover the more narrow compliance exercise.

Part 2.
Responding to Risks

2.1. Responding to Risk: Managing Options, Finding Balance, Creating Levers

Risk to operations management cycle

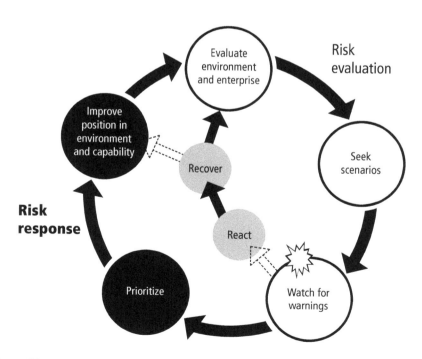

Figure 17

"I view managing operational risk in much the same light that I view quality control. If it is an after-the-fact, defensive component of the process, then it is less effective than if it is an important component of how the organization does business and is built into the process at the front end. In other words, operational risk management should be a part of how an organization defines its operating philosophy."

— *Mark Olson*

In risk evaluation, *watch for warnings* illuminated the state of the enterprise in terms of environment and capabilities. The watching was in the context of scenarios for understanding possible risks. This is the launching point for risk response. Now, we turn to *risk response*, the second half of the cycle we've been using. This part of the cycle aims to help an institution prioritize improvements, build capability, reposition in the environment, and, when needed, use plan B to react and recover.

In public and private discussions, operational risk leaders who report progress in finding and evaluating risks still struggle with responding to risks. While reasons vary, they describe similar symptoms in an organization:

- a backlog of risks to fix

- the difficulty of assembling business cases for proposed responses

- slow responses to an unfolding chain of events

- the reappearance of 'bad things' that are never fully resolved

- insufficient ability to take advantage of environment changes to seize business opportunity.

Focus on basics to avoid stumbling blocks

In the chapter on watching for warnings (1.10), the example of a boat in a storm helped make the distinction between warnings about the environment and warnings about capabilities. This example continues to help as we add the implications of quality of planning and available time.

Time creates and forecloses options for action

In the shorter term, planning can be undertaken to deal with factors in the environment, for example, to head back into port if the weather starts to turn bad. And likewise for capability factors; for example, to put a bucket in the boat in case we need to bail out water.

In the longer term, planning can be done to add capabilities (in oversight, management, controls and core processes) to make the boat better able to sail in rougher seas or reposition in the environment (ports and routes) so the boat can sail in smooth seas elsewhere instead.

This also applies to risks such as fraud, trading and business continuity. For example, as will be discussed in chapter 2.5 on product management and fraud prevention, better planning for fraud-related scenarios in product management is a solid path to prevention.

It is key to explicitly recognize that:

- different time horizons have different response options in planning, environment and capabilities

- there are trade-offs between planning, environment and capabilities.

To apply these basics to more easily shift from compliance to a performance-driven, systematic approach, start by focusing on the business objectives.

Business objectives drive key actions

- *In responding to risk, our business objective* is to improve risk-adjusted return by *reducing risk to return*. In a metrics sense, this is improving risk-adjusted return. Practically, the test is whether *action is taken* on problems previously identified.

- Taking that action more efficiently and effectively is easier with a focus on key points.

- In responding to risk, understand your range of options, the cost of the options and the value of keeping them open to respond to risk. Scrutinize decisions that would foreclose your options to prevent or react to risk.

- Time matters—understand the implications at each step of the cycle.

- Take advantage of the wide range of proven approaches to reduce risk from disciplines such as business process improvement/reengineering, quality control, software application development, business continuity, crisis management, strategic planning and financial management.

- Select from the range of tools/techniques to help clarify risk-response priorities for action.

- Tools are ways to make capability improvement easier. Capability improvements are levers (in both the risk management and competitive strategy senses) for outcome improvements. Create levers!

- Make a distinction between response to risks that are environment-related (usually external and non-process driven), and those that are process-related.

- Make a distinction between strengthening capabilities in oversight, management, controls and the business product process (analyze, develop, market, sell, deliver, support).

- Partner with other teams in the institution with objectives to improve process, grow profitable revenue and/or protect from risk.

- Efficient and effective 'command and control' capabilities are crucial to being able to react fast enough to minimize loss or take advantage of opportunity.

- Once a problem arises, the focus is on slowing or stopping the cascade of events to reduce the impact and consequences. Success in this reduction is dependent on underlying business process capability, preparedness, controls and early warning situational awareness.

- Rapid recovery largely depends on quickly finding the root cause of the change, understanding the environment and/or process, and advanced preparations for recovery.

- Improvements over the longer term are the only true way to risk reduction. Heroic, shorter-term fixes are needed to stay in business, but efficient risk response depends on improvements in capabilities and positioning within or reshaping the environment.

- Understanding controls in basic terms makes it easier to make controls more effective in finding and fixing problems, as well as helping in rendering them more efficient to implement, maintain and test.

- Product management discipline can help engage an institution to reduce a range of risks, such as fraud, while improving business outcomes.

- Information technology risk grows as institutions become more dependent on technology. Established tools can help you map dependencies, and avoid product and process problems.

- Your opportunity as an operational risk leader is to harness the range of proven tools and engage well-trained people to: 1) use risk management insight to apply this capability to the top priorities for risk reduction and 2) lead the team to solutions that are faster, better and cheaper than would have occurred otherwise. This creates shareholder value.

Applying these key points is our focus in the remainder of this chapter and the next several:

2.2—Prioritizing Improvements

2.3—Strengthening the Institution in its Environment

2.4—Improving Control Capability

2.5—Improving Product Management and Fraud Prevention

2.6—Improving IT-related Business Risk Management

2.7—React and Recover—Right Action at the Right Time

2.8—Key Insights for Responding to Risk

Responding to risk essentials

As a preview, recall the two loops in the risk management cycle:

1. The steady-state cycle includes prioritizing improvements in capability and/or positioning within the environment. This includes *planning in advance* to reduce the likelihood of a chain of events from unfolding and to mitigate its impact if it happens.

2. The exception cycle reacts to a situation and then recovers.

The two loops are recommended because they have proven history in a variety of settings and can help you collaborate with professionals from various risk disciplines. For example, the steady-state cycle is more familiar to process-improvement professionals. The reaction cycle is more familiar to security, continuity and hazard risk professionals.

Classic risk-response categories are: avoid completely; share/transfer; mitigate/reduce/treat; and accept/tolerate completely.

Avoid completely and accept/tolerate completely are straightforward.

Share/transfer includes several arrangements:

- financial sharing: insurance

- operational sharing: contract to a third party (e.g. outsourcing)

- financial and operational sharing: contract to third party with financial recourse/indemnification.

In all of these, the prime party is still legally responsible for the risk and can feel financial repercussions through contractual penalties from customers, regulatory fines and judicial judgments.

Mitigate/reduce is the focus of our discussion on reducing risk. In particular, to help reduce risk in a way that a) drives business performance, b) is efficient, and c) demonstrates the business benefit of the operational risk management function.

Each involves repositioning or reshaping (avoid being the extreme case), or otherwise improving capability. Or, indeed, both.

Using proven tools

In addition to these classic risk-response (sometimes called 'risk treatment') categories, there is also a body of proven tools and approaches for reducing risk to return.

These tools and approaches come from disciplines such as operations research; business process reengineering/improvement; quality control/improvement; information technology management; business continuity; project management; facilities management; strategy; product management; and finance. Many, if not all, can be found inside financial institutions and (in other flavors) in a range of industries.

These tools and approaches are much the same as those encountered in risk evaluation. Here the aspects applicable to responding to risk are used.

Using the right tool for the risk

In this discussion of responding to risk, the *focus is on the role of the operational risk leader* in leveraging these proven tools and approaches, especially in the context of an extended (matrixed) operational risk management team. And to do so within an institution to improve performance and compliance.

As these tools have multiple applications, **what is important to the operational risk leader is to be able to associate a particular risk situation with a tool to provide initial focus to a risk-response-planning team**. This is simpler if the risk situations can be grouped in ways that point to categories of risk response approaches.

To do this, we can think of the *sources of change* (for better or worse) in two big categories:

1. **Environment.** Examples include economic, political, social, competitive, market and natural conditions, and malicious activities such as cyber or physical attacks. These are more dynamic threats that require readiness to react when a cascade of events is unleashed.

2. **Enterprise capability.** This includes changes in oversight, management, control and core process capabilities that (as changes do) open gaps that weaken ability to act/react as the environment changes. Examples include problems in product process (including extended enterprise processes that connect with partners and customers), trading processes (the mechanics, but not changes in prices) and frauds that exploit process weaknesses.

Risk response types vary with change source and impact

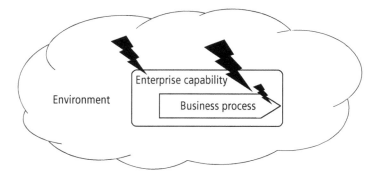

Figure 18

Making this distinction means we can reach into the toolbox to draw on the most appropriate tools for the job.

This helps save time and money. **Fixing weaknesses in business processes is usually more cost-effective and reliable in the face of a range of threats than just layering on more controls and audits**.

With this as a starting point, we next turn to the steps of the risk-response process, starting with prioritizing improvements.

Operational risk leader difference

Your personal opportunity is to:

Manage options

Understand the business value of your options to act. The value of knowing now, rather than later. The value of acting now, rather than later—having more time to act. The value of having several response options, rather than being forced into one.

Financial option theory applies here. What would you pay to get more information on the situation? What would you pay to be able to contain your risk at a particular point in a cascade, such as a fraud, supply chain disruption from earthquake or flood, information systems failure or robo-signings of foreclosure documents?

In particular, focus analysis and resources on irreversible decisions— especially when time matters most. This is one of the many insights stressed by Peter Bernstein in his book, *Against the Gods: The Remarkable Story of Risk*.[23]

Options are crucial in real-world operational incident management. There are two general types of response plans.

1. In highly standardized and predictable chains of events, detailed response procedures can be specified, e.g. 'Push the off button' or an IT system restoration checklist.

2. However, if unfolding events are more complex and/or we know less, then the response must be more broad and flexible to provide options. These situations stress the need for pre-planned decision criteria and resources. When trouble strikes, a generalized response plan is tailored to the immediate problem situation.

This is a key distinction. Confusing these two types of plans can make a situation worse when it is time to act.

Find balance

With the tools known, your personal difference is finding the right balance between responding and waiting. This comes up at each step in the risk response process. For example, the right amount of preparation, training, controls; the right time to react (how much 'wait and see'); or the right order of risk root causes to fix. Your leadership matters in helping the organization make a better decision thanks to the people you engaged, and information you framed and provided without delay.

Create levers

Tools make it easier to create capabilities (not only for risk management, but also for competitive strategy and other areas). These capabilities are levers to push to reduce real risk to return in the business. More efficient and effective levers are key to success.

---

[23] Bernstein, Peter L. (1996), *Against the Gods: The Remarkable Story of Risk*. (Hoboken: Wiley & Sons).

Use these tools to help your extended team **design and implement better
solutions that reduce risk to business performance objectives**.

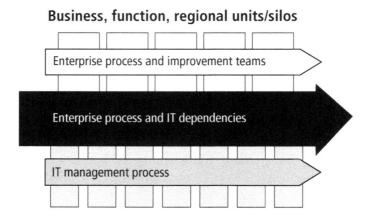

Figure 19

Designing better solutions helps overcome objections that reducing risks is
just too costly. Your skill at inviting the right people (who also care about
improving business product processes) to the discussion is powerful. This
way you not only create a more workable solution to the immediate risk, but
also solve other problems that spring from the same root causes. Of course,
the danger in trying to solve too many problems at once is the 'boiling the
ocean' syndrome. To avoid this, create several cost/benefit financial cases (of
course, risk adjust these costs and benefits!). This will help the team land on
a consensus and provide a more powerful business case.

> **Tip**: Remember, operating management owns risk. However, you are the one with
> the big picture of risks and options. Your role is to facilitate a discussion that brings
> the greatest risk–return business value.

Key points

- There are two loops to the risk-response cycle—steady state and immediate reaction. Both are sensitive to time.

- Risk-response actions are more efficient and effective when focused on business objectives.

- As a leader, understand the business value of your options to act, and do it sooner rather than later.

2.2. Prioritizing Improvements

Risk to operations management cycle

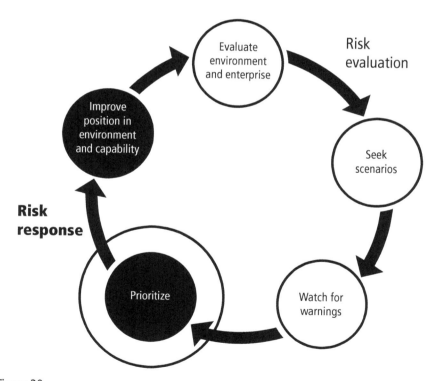

Figure 20

"There are no quick fixes. You need to focus on structural fixes and changes. Try to transform your organization in meaningful ways. Two keys to this are, first, understanding deeply the system that is your bank, how that works; and second, the root causes that can hurt your system. If you know this, you can point your analytics at the right data. This is what I expect my risk management leaders to understand—the business."

— **Humphrey Polanen**

In our discussion of evaluating risk, a systematic, scenario-based approach was taken to avoid bad surprises. Yet, after a series of scenario-analysis workshops, managers typically ask, 'What do we do first?' After thinking about options, they add: 'And, how do we decide—both in view of the evaluation and the potential response(s)?' **Not every risk requires action. There is a cost/benefit balance. At the same time, the systems view of risks shines a light on the full frequency and magnitude of losses associated with a risk. This 'full cost' view can make a more compelling cost/benefit case to act.**

Prioritizing improvement—capability areas and criteria

Improvements can be made in each of four areas that work together for the business to make informed, risk–return balanced decisions to create value for shareholders:

1. core business product process

2. controls

3. management

4. oversight (governance).

There are trade-offs between making improvements in each area. For example, controls can compensate for poor process, but often at excessive cost compared to fixing the process. Each has to work reasonably well or the enterprise will suffer. For example, one institution was highly efficient in information technology. Yet business leaders complained that spending priorities were wrong—oversight was inadequate. Environment adjustments are in the oversight and management categories as decisions are made there to enter and exit markets, products and geographic areas.

Limited resources require choices. Yet, recall the guidance of quality expert Philip Crosby—"Quality is Free." Quality is about how closely the outcome conforms to an objective; risk management makes it easier to achieve quality. Better risk management (especially in process-oriented operational risks) should save cost. So our risk-response actions (aside from those compliance mandates that have no business value to shareholders, customers or partners), should also be free (where 'free' means paid for by new revenue or cost savings)—whether in terms of immediate savings from reducing process-related risks or benefits from addressing risks that rarely unfold.

There are generally three criteria to prioritize:

- mandates—legal, regulatory, contract and policy requirements

- importance (frequency multiplied by impact) of risks insufficiently addressed at a point in time [24]

- efficiency and effectiveness in two senses—risk management as an overall process and managing a specific risk.

> **Tip**: Establishing priorities can be complicated when organizations often find themselves confused about what to prioritize in the face of varying types of improvements and reasons to do so. Don't fall into this trap.

Make it simpler: evaluate potential improvements with a three-by-three matrix. Rows are the four areas and columns are the three criteria.

	MANDATES	IMPORTANCE	EFFICIENCY AND EFFECTIVENESS
Core process			
Controls			
Management			
Oversight			

Set priorities with balance across each of the four areas. Without balance, resources will be wasted. For example, overemphasis on fixing the core product cycle tends to be misdirected because there are insufficient 'headlights' from risk oversight and risk management to prioritize the core process improvements. Or overemphasis on risk management (that is, by the

---

[24] Your team members with quality control experience may multiply this by a score for ability to detect. This is referred to as a 'risk prioritization number'.

risk management team without engaging other experts in the business) tends to generate either a) risks identified in the more 'known' areas of core process with gaps in the less 'known' areas; or b) a long list of findings without fixes to actually reduce risk to share value.

Visualizing priorities—tools to make it easier

We now turn to a tour of tools to make it easier to visualize priorities. Please note that a) there are variations on each of these tools and b) they can be applied at multiple points in the risk management cycle (after a rough view of a risk, a more carefully analyzed view of risk, a quick response solution outline or a more carefully designed response solution).

Risk tolerance analysis

When the board defines a willingness (sometimes called an 'appetite') to take risk in pursuit of return across an enterprise, or by business line, product, functional area or geographic region, they specify some criteria.[25] Then the risk amounts are allocated to the subsidiary risks within those areas.

Risk limits can be specified in one of two ways:

1. An *absolute limit*, with one or more warning zones leading up to the stop point.

2. A target risk with one or more warning zones. This is more frequently used when only one direction is 'bad' (personal injury is always bad). When the risk strays from the target to the boundary of the warning zone that is the *absolute limit*. This is can be used when two directions are 'bad' (as in recording a customer's investment preferences as either too conservative or too aggressive).

Either produces the same focus on the absolute limit. Using and communicating a consistent approach is helpful.

A risk tolerance analysis prioritizes those items that are most in danger of breaching the limit.

---

[25] Because use of risk terminology varies among professional disciplines, please note that in this book, 'risk appetite' refers to the amount of risk an enterprise is willing to accept in pursuit of its objectives. 'Risk tolerance' refers to the acceptable variation around the desired amount of risk (appetite). Exceeding the range is known as being 'out of tolerance'.

The limitation of this tool is that the magnitude of the impact (including cascades and consequences) of the event flow does not easily jump out of the analysis.

The technique is generally most helpful for focusing on the likelihood of breach when impact is clearer—such as performance of transaction-processing systems.

Frequency-impact heat maps

Probably the most basic of risk management graphic tools is the heat map—a plot of frequency against impact. The more important items float to the upper right corner of the plot. They are scaled in several ways, such as impact being scaled by the loss of a year of net income. The charts are often color-coded moving toward deeper shades of red toward the upper right corner to reinforce the 'heat' concept. The size and shape of the bands reflect an institution's willingness to take risk and relative concerns about frequency compared to impact. For example, the following diagram is drawn to reflect an institution that is sensitive to high impact situations.

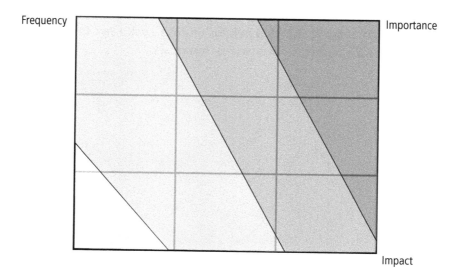

Figure 21

Limitations

Any two-factor chart is limited to that information. In addition, there are other limitations:

- First, the 'risks' plotted need common definition based on the real risk scenarios created earlier. Too often, data points are a jumble of actors, objects, actions, impacts and consequences.

- Second, once the points are comparable, they need to be comparably stated in terms of the frequency and impact they reflect. This is not only using common scales or qualitative description, but also measured at a comparable stage of an unfolding chain of events, otherwise costs won't be comparable.

- Third, as a quick summary tool, the chart hides critical information—the distribution of the frequency and impact of each data point. It only plots average frequency against average impact—it doesn't reflect distributions. Averages are by definition below 'worst case'. When only averages are plotted, rather than distributions, organizations are often surprised when something bad happens—and that should be no surprise.

To see the detail, the frequency, impact and combined probability, distributions should be reviewed to visually see how the losses for a risk type behave and compare to others. Look for outliers—ask *why*? Outlier causes can point to KRIs and cost-effective risk responses.

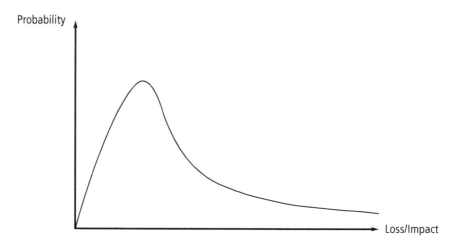

Figure 22

For our purposes of a simple tool to make it easier to visualize priorities, an easy improvement helps overcome this limitation. For each risk data point, add a shaded area as a *rough* reflection of a *portion* of the distribution of probability and impact. The dots are the averages. The shaded areas make it easier to see the nature of each item. If data is available, the shape of the area can be made more precise. For example, circles suggest normal distributions. Right triangles suggest long-tailed distributions. Rectangles suggest, uncertainty and/or broadly defined items. Within the limitations of the tool, the key to helpfulness is comparable reflection of real risk behavior. For example, it often becomes clear that there are few high-frequency and high-impact situations (if there are, the institution is in serious trouble). This helps foster conversation on causes and focuses priorities. Examples are rough illustrative only.

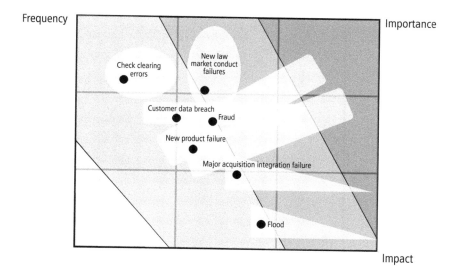

Figure 23

Another limitation is often in interpretation. More than one risk manager has been derailed in an executive meeting when a business executive looks at the upper right quadrant of the graphic (the area of greatest impact and frequency) and exclaims: 'We already paid for that, it's no longer a problem!'

Improvements

One approach to avoid such executive critiques, often already followed by diligent risk managers, is to show the frequency and impact in the current state after applying previously identified improvements. However, this doesn't visually 'jump out' well or express organizational focus.

A better approach sometimes is to combine frequency and impact on the vertical axis and name it 'importance.' On the now-available horizontal axis, plot the gap between current state and desired state. Here the states are numbered, say, 0 through 5 (5 being the best) and the current number is subtracted from the desired number, leaving the gap—which is what you plot on the graph. Then the high priority-high gap items are highlighted in the upper right. Thinking about capabilities is helpful because it forces consideration of root causes that affect capabilities.

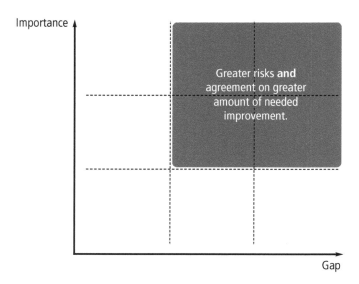

Figure 24

Tip: Do this with your cross-unit workshop team and key executives individually and then share the combined organizational view in a cross-organization executive meeting. **This can help engage the organization more deeply, surfacing differences, and building shared priorities and action**.

Cost/benefit analysis

This tool is used in many areas. In applying it to risk management, a few adjustments are made.

- In 'benefits' include both loss avoided and opportunity gained. Use frequency multiplied by impact to quantify and count the range of benefits from the response (for example, business product process improvement to reduce fraud or know-your-customer compliance improvement can also improve process efficiency and cross-sell/up-sell to customers). Review the business process flow and dependency analysis conducted in the risk evaluation steps to quickly spot benefits that might be missed.

- In 'costs' include costs necessary to achieve benefits, but which might appear in different budgets within an institution, such as information technology costs. When counting costs, follow your existing financial policy for costs that will generate benefits in other projects (such as an improved user-access management system).

- If the benefits or costs extend beyond the current accounting period, apply net present value.

Prioritize based on excess of benefits over cost.

Limitations

Even with these adjustments, mandated improvements (by law, regulation, contract or policy) that must be implemented will eat into the budget available to prioritize on a cost/benefit basis.

It is difficult to visualize the risk implications in traditional graphics with cost on one axis and benefit on the other.

Improvements

In addition to the adjustments above, the graphics can be improved to show benefit/cost on one axis and importance (frequency multiplied by impact) on the other. This allows risk responses strong on both dimensions to float to the upper right of the diagram.

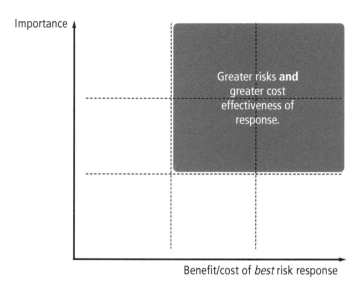

Figure 25

> **Tip**: Be clear in whether cost/benefit analysis is before or after consideration of the risk response solution design. Too often, poor solution designs are excessively costly or produce insufficient benefits. In such cases an institution will exit an activity or just accept the risk without action. Both of these are sub-optimal. As discussed below, the preferred approach is more intelligent solution design based on solid scenario analysis.

Detection-impact-frequency analysis

This tool is found frequently in the quality control world. It can be referred to as a 'blindside chart' because **it highlights risks that could blindside your organization because of a lack of ability to see such risk events unfolding**. It goes beyond the basic frequency-multiplied-by-impact heat map to add another dimension—the ability to detect a problem.

Industries such as aviation, manufacturing and healthcare always want to 'turn the lights on' in this way. They know that if they can't see (i.e. detect) a problem, they cannot take action to prevent or reduce it.

To create the chart, whether in a table of numbers or visual graph, the ability to detect is added. In a graph, one axis is importance (frequency multiplied by impact). The other axis is the lack of ability to detect (so that the worse ability to detect is away from the graph origin). In this way, the upper right quadrant of the diagram prioritizes the most unclear and important items.

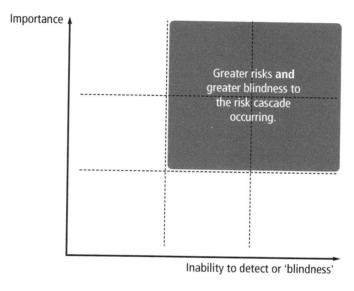

Figure 26

Risk budget

Risk budget is a simple yet powerful tool that works especially well in communicating with the finance organization and engaging executives accountable for risks. This is partially because it starts with a familiar tool in the organization—approval worksheets for new projects.

To create a risk budget, the operational risk manager works with the financial-planning team to simply add four columns to the typical project budget spreadsheet:

Column 1: Frequency multiplied by the impact of the risk of *that project line* (e.g. customer take rate, repeat sales, customer churn rate, IT systems availability, expected fraud, or support costs per support channel [branch, teleservices, web, mobile]). For impact, consider the average and more severe cases, as reflected in a loss distribution (to whatever extent it is available).

111

Column 2: Rating of the understanding of the risk. This could be as simple as 'high', 'medium' or 'low' or may be a more quantitative score.

Column 3: Expected costs of reducing that risk (e.g. improved marketing, more reliable IT systems, adding more features to a software application, or better employee training).

Column 4: Rating of the understanding of the risk response. How certain are we that it is the right response, designed the right way and will be implemented as expected? This could be as simple as 'high', 'medium' or 'low' or may be a more quantitative score.

The risk and finance teams drive a discussion with all parties to determine if the organization understands the risk and response, if the risk is acceptable, and whether to allocate resources to reduce risk. For example, the team may wish to improve the user experience of a software application to retain customers, as the risk reduction benefit from this is more certain than from additional marketing.

This discussion must be meaningful; it should not be simply a perfunctory risk discussion of the usual suspects.

Risk-response knowledge matrix

This is a tool that is part of the risk budget, but it can also be used on its own. It is simply a two-dimensional chart with knowledge of the nature of the risk ('What could happen?'—how important, large, frequent, well understood is it?) on one axis and knowledge of the response ('What would we do?'—is our solution well-understood, good quality and do we know how much skill, time and cost it will take to implement?) on the other. In an executive interview or risk workshop with representatives from various areas of the institution, team members are asked to plot risks on the chart.

Level of knowledge can be used to prioritize opportunities

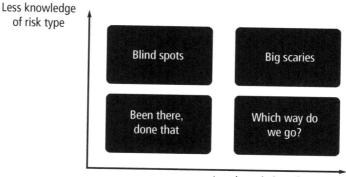

Figure 27

These two dimensions are much more powerful than asking executives: 'What are your top three risks?'

In workshops engaging people with multiple perspectives, **it creates a fascinating discussion when what is obvious to one person is a mystery to another**. With many major losses, there are often lonely voices who were sounding an alarm in advance. This tool can help make those voices heard.

Hazard totem pole

Developed from the safety and hazard risk management disciplines, the hazard totem pole is another powerful and simple diagram. Each risk is a layer in a pyramid graphic. The greater risks are at the top. Starting at the top, resources are allocated to eliminate or control risks, stopping at either a 'safe enough' evaluation or a cost/benefit balance point.[26]

---

[26] The hazard totem pole is one of several techniques developed by Vernon Grose and published in his 1987 book *Managing Risk: Systematic Loss Prevention for Executives* (Prentice Hall).

Risk-response type matrix

This simple tool focuses on efficiency in risk response.

The rows of the matrix list risks. The columns list responses.

'X' marks the spot for each response appropriate for a risk type. Visually, the columns with the most 'X's tend to be the most efficient.

Limitations

The basic matrix does not weigh the risks or the costs of the responses.

Improvements

The risks can be listed on rows based on importance. The 'X's can be replaced with cost values or color coding.

Simple risk-response matrix

Look for 'high-power' responses that can fix root causes in multiple risk types. These have high cost/benefit value.

	Response 1	Response 2	Response 3	Response 4	Response 5	Response 6	Response n
Risk 1	●			●			
Risk 2		●					
Risk 3			●	●		●	
Risk 4			●		●		
Risk 5			●				
Risk 6							●
Risk n					●		

Figure 28

Risk-response exercises, tests or audits

An entire category of tools provides more realism to the workshop-style evaluations. These tests include managerial self-testing, audits or regulatory examinations.

The testing can be as simple as a review of paperwork or tabletop simulations, or may range up to mock disaster-planning exercises. Some excellent guidance (including detailed sample materials) is available at **www.fema.gov**, the website of the US Federal Emergency Management Agency. For business continuity purposes, the US Federal Financial Institutions Examination Council specifies the use of more rigorous exercises in their *Examination Handbook* (**www.ffiec.gov**).

Concluding thoughts

Prioritization tools combine an understanding of root cause with needed solutions to point to top areas for action. Different tools emphasize different criteria. Select the appropriate tool for the circumstances. The objective is investing wisely in improvements that enable your institution to more safely pursue return.

Key points

- Risk-response knowledge charts create fascinating discussions when what is obvious to one person is a mystery to others.

- Improved heat maps help engage the organization, surfacing differences and building shared priorities.

- Project risk discussions must be meaningful, not perfunctory discussions of the 'usual suspects'.

2.3. Strengthening the Institution in its Environment

Risk to operations management cycle

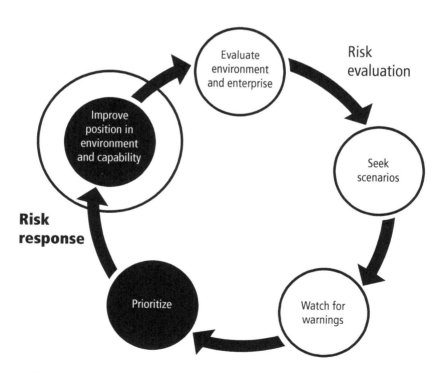

Figure 29

"If you want to make real improvements in business performance, you must address the quality of business processes, including the talent and organization of people doing the work. So we understand the quality of the core processes and controls in each organizational unit, including training, quality of staff, quality of management, adequacy of financial controls, and other capability measures. The better the quality of your processes and controls, the lower your operational risk in any area."

— *Ron Dietz*

Knowledge of the environment and enterprise capabilities enabled us **to create realistic, systematic 'What if?' scenarios with an integrated view across risks**. Knowledge of real root cause in cascading situations enabled us to know what to watch for warnings. Knowledge of scenarios, warning signs, and appropriate tools enabled us to pick the right priorities for improvement.

Finalizing priorities covers both the frequency and impact of a risk, and the costs of the solution. Because well-designed solutions provide many benefits by fixing a few root causes, the importance of inclusive business cases was discussed—to see the full benefit and apportion costs among the areas that benefit. In this way, **benefits include better prevention and preparedness, lower cost, better service, and greater flexibility for revenue—in other words, improved business performance**.

In workshops, it is at this point when a manager normally asks me: 'We're strengthening our evaluation. But how do we add value in substantive improvements?' The answer is in the question. The operational risk team has brought together a wide range of insights in scenario analysis and focused on priorities: This can help the team facilitate better solutions. Of course, it's always best to build an operational risk management team with people who know the business. The foundation of risk evaluation was understanding the environment and enterprise. These are also the two areas of improvement.

In facing the environment, an enterprise can either reposition to achieve a better risk/return balance (for example, exit a product line, enter certain geographic markets, reduce supply chain reliance on earthquake-prone areas, or move a data center out of a flood zone) or seek to reshape the environment (for example, participate in coalitions to improve the use of technology, stimulate local economic development or lobby policy makers). These are excellent opportunities to team up with strategy, product management, and business continuity colleagues.

In strengthening capabilities, improvements to improve robustness, resilience or margin for accommodating problems can be made in oversight, management, controls and core processes:

- **Oversight/Governance**: Oversight/governance is about getting the right information to the right people at the right time to make the right (or at least better) decisions and to do so with accountability. In the corporate or broad business sense, this is beyond the scope of this book. However, key issues in risk oversight will be addressed.

- **Management**: Management here applies to all management capability in the institution. This book addresses the intersection of risk and operations management.

- **Controls**: For many, controls are just one aspect of management. Here, because of the regulatory focus and the significant opportunity for improvement, they will be the focus of chapter 2.4.

- **Core processes**: Institutions earn a profit from customers by providing products and services. They are the engine of the enterprise.

Two examples follow in chapters 2.5 and 2.6, based on the pressing needs of managers with whom I speak. The first relates to the product management process, because it drives revenue and is a key opportunity to reduce fraud. The second covers dependencies on information technology.

Two points have helped others:

1. Be clear on trade-offs between improvements. For example, you could fix the branch banking deposit automated system or layer on more human controls. In the short term, you might be willing to tolerate the cost of those layers of controls, but a longer-term automated solution is less expensive for operating and continuously monitoring the controls. Importantly, broken processes can't be fixed with controls or investigations. Thus, the root cause in the process must ultimately be fixed.

2. Don't be trapped by tunnel vision—seeing only limited options for improvement. Make your life easier and keep using your scenarios. Whether an event chain is related to the environment (e.g. hurricane) or process (e.g. fraud or product failure), responses can be better understood in the context of why and how fast a problem can arise.

2.4. Improving Control Capability

First step to control efficiency—clarity

A control has a range of definitions from different disciplines, including the range covered by operational risk. Some state what a control does. Others state the benefits. In an attempt to bridge some of the differences, this functional definition is offered: **A 'control' measures conformance with specification, and then acts on that information** (reports, protects, alters, corrects). Even simpler, controls can be said to *detect and act* or *sense and respond*. Some controls only report a status; others are smarter and take rule-driven actions based on a policy.[27] To make it easier to fix problems and simplify controls, it is helpful to distinguish controls from policies (principles and objectives), procedures, and rules—especially those that address non-process causes. For example, a policy statement to employees on bribery is very different from rules in software that validate payees and the purposes of payments.

The benefit from a control is greater when it is located at a level where it can point to the problem, stop it or at least provide a start on the fix.

Controls are often described as 'preventative', 'predictive', 'detective', or 'corrective'. However, this is simplified by stating where a control is located in a business process flow relative to a problem and its decision-rule capability.

---

[27] This definition comes from operations and general *management* disciplines. *Assurance* perspectives tend to be more broad: 'Any action taken by management, the board, and other parties ...'

Controls in unfolding events...

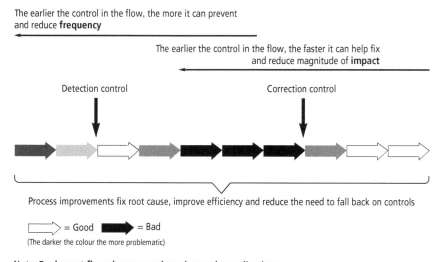

The earlier the control in the flow, the more it can prevent
and reduce **frequency**

The earlier the control in the flow, the faster it can help fix
and reduce magnitude of **impact**

Detection control   Correction control

Process improvements fix root cause, improve efficiency and reduce the need to fall back on controls

☐⇒ = Good ■■▶ = Bad
(The darker the colour the more problematic)

Note: Real event flows have many branches and complications.

Figure 30

In the diagram—highly simplified—the problem is in the middle of the process flow. If a control is before the problem, it is detective relative to the problem. It might also be corrective relative to an upstream event.

As indicated by the arrows, the farther in front of the problem (and closer to cause), then the more preventative the control is of the problem. These are relative concepts. Making controls more efficient and effective has much to do with the placement of the control to be able to quickly identify root cause and fix it.

Testing controls—who does what?

Controls are tested from several organizational perspectives. When these aren't clear, waste and confusion arise from multiple teams testing at multiple times and to multiple criteria. Clarity on two basic points helps.

First, six organizational perspectives are commonly used: business-management assessment; risk management team assessment; internal-control review; internal audit; external audit; and regulatory examination. Depending on the organization, the first two or three are considered managerial. The others are assurance.

Tip: Make the process more efficient and effective

1. Encourage a culture that emphasizes the managerial reviews. This promotes managerial ownership, leads to improvements made faster and reduces negative surprises in the assurance reviews.

2. Create clarity in the benchmarks to avoid confusion across reviews. This also provides an opportunity to evaluate to a higher standard in managerial reviews so as to drive improvement.

Second, design, implementation and operation (including maintenance) of controls is tested.

The design of the control needs to be appropriate for the position of the control relative to the business process being controlled. Can it detect root case? Provide early warning? Reduce or slow the impact of an adverse event? Then it needs to be implemented properly to function as designed.

The operation of the control needs to achieve the performance or compliance objective defined in the design both efficiently and effectively. This is also probed with questions such as: Is it reliable? Is it used, or is it circumvented informally, or frequently formally overridden? Is it cost/benefit-effective? Is it maintained?

To make operational testing more efficient, continuous controls monitoring is gaining attention. The two key sources of guidance on this are from The Institute of Internal Auditors and ISACA.[28] This guidance includes efficiency and effectiveness, avoiding gaps and understanding distinctions in various levels of assurance (both in test quality and in the depth of what is actually tested in the layers of the IT system). Both organizations provide extensive guidance on controls in general.

---

[28] The IIA's GTAG 'Guide 3: Continuous Auditing: Implications for Assurance, Monitoring, and Risk Assessment' is no charge for members (**www.theiia.org/guidance/technology/gtag3**). ISACA's 'Monitoring Internal Control Systems and IT' (**bit.ly/d8Il55**) is no charge for members.

Toward more effective self-assessments

When management performs the assessment of their own controls, this is a self-assessment (as opposed to an independent assessment).

RCSAs are one of the basic tools of operational risk. Everyone uses them and most struggle with them. Ask five people at a conference and you'll find that even the name isn't uniform—risk and control self-assessment; risk control self-assessment; control self-assessment. A scan of regulatory documents also reveals different definitions. Despite these challenges, RCSAs can quickly become more efficient and effective when they are seen as one step in a risk management cycle. This is especially important for those institutions using RCSAs in incentive compensation.

To avoid problems, ask yourself five key questions:

1. **Do we first 'know the business'**? Many assessments are focused only on known risks, controls and weaknesses (proverbial watched pots). They miss weaknesses that are less apparent and those in the underlying process.

2. How sound was the risk evaluation that led to the controls being designed and implemented? **Assessments depend on properly completed prior steps in risk evaluation and response**—including environment and enterprise capability evaluation; scenario analysis; root-cause analysis; dependency analysis; control design and control implementation. If any of that was unsound, then it is likely the wrong controls are assessed and findings have little value.

3. Does the assessment cycle **keep pace with real-world change**? If change in risks (environment and process, or controls) is more frequent than the evaluation period, then assessments will miss real risk. For example, if your IT environment changes every few months, then business-continuity test cycles should match that cycle—anything else gives a false sense of confidence.

4. Do control assessments **actually focus on controls** or do they mix in policies, procedures or rules? The existence of policies is a long way from examining a control that can detect out-of-bounds conditions and act on that information.

5. Do assessments divert attention from **daily *use* of risk management**? Both lag time and emphasis on control (rather than environment or

business capabilities) have a tendency to cause organizations to see risk management as only a bandage, assurance function, rather than a valued management function that fixes root causes.

If they fall into the traps above, then such risk or control assessments probably also divert resources from more helpful risk management activities and create a false sense of assurance. These traps have led to serious harm. Consider data breaches, frauds, network outages, robo-signings and other problems that occurred when controls were – on paper –acceptable.[29]

Another key to success is the rigor with which the tests are applied to both the design and operation of controls, in view of the risks in the environment and enterprise capabilities. Will your car break down on your family vacation? How closely will you look at the condition of the car? Put air in the tires? Check fluids? Computer diagnostic? Get a tune-up? Conduct scheduled maintenance?

To avoid traps, five helpful evaluation questions are:

- **Does management really own the assessment and want to improve**? If a third party (e.g. internal control) conducts the assessment (without addressing the other traps and assumptions) and management has little involvement or use, then paperwork will provide little performance value to shareholders.

- **Who is asked**? Ask people close to the *business process being controlled*. Reviews of many incidents reveal that someone, somewhere, knew. Your job—before something bad happens—is to ask the most knowledgeable person(s) so as to find that voice. Scenario analysis should help point to the right people.

- **What is asked**? Probe with questions that flow from the control design document. Focus on the *control objectives in support of specific business objectives* (revenue, cost, efficiency, effectiveness, customer satisfaction, compliance).

- **What benchmark is used**? Numerical 1–5, 1–7 or 1–10 scales can be subjective. Anchor the numerical values (at least most of them) with some statement of what that number means. Ensure this is clear to all respondents.

- **Do questions avoid bias**? Using both the specific business objectives and the numerical ratings with explanations, structure the questions to help

---

[29] A helpful commentary on RCSAs is provided in *A New Approach for Managing Operational Risk*, Society of Actuaries, Revised, 2010.

avoid bias; for example, tying questions about controls on new product launches directly to the steps in the new product process.

The first set of questions stressed the prerequisites that must be in place for an RCSA to provide meaningful results. The second set of questions stressed the need to tie to control objectives that then tie to business outcomes. **The common and simple failure to look at what comes before and after RCSAs in a risk management cycle has wasted much in the way of resources and given many institutions a wholly false sense of security**. The good news is that it is relatively easy to fix. Fixing makes it a more reliable input to incentive compensation.

Plenty of guidance on the subject of self-assessments is available. Among these, the Collaborative Assurance & Risk Design (CARD) is one of the more robust. It was created by Tim Leech, one of the distinguished OCEG fellows and frequent writer on assessments. This approach is helpful because, while focused on financial reporting, it embraces industrial-style control evaluation to create more insight from the time and effort spent in the assessments.[30]

Improving through automation

Once the RCSA is refined in the context of its position in the risk management cycle, **controls testing can be improved through automation**.

This automation can be used for periodic testing of controls and the underlying transactions (often termed 'computer-assisted audit tools') or for continuous monitoring of those controls and underlying transactions (often termed 'continuous controls monitoring', 'continuous transaction monitoring', 'transaction monitoring' or 'continuous monitoring'). In addition, continuous auditing (CA) is used to fulfill assurance requirements.

Earlier it was observed that resources can be devoted to fixing the underlying transactions or to layering on controls and monitoring them. Generally, it is more efficient to just fix the transaction process. To provide more frequent (and hopefully effective) and efficient assurance, continuous automation support is used.

---

[30] More information can be found at **bit.ly/9hzMya**. Look for papers on self-assessment.

Three layers of continuous automation support

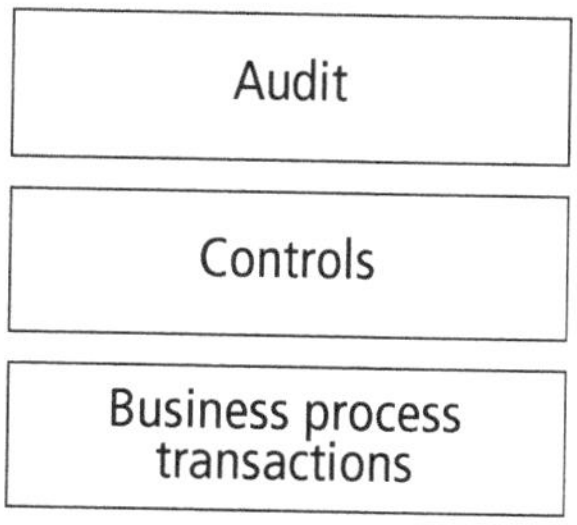

```
┌─────────────────────────────────┐
│             Audit               │
└─────────────────────────────────┘
┌─────────────────────────────────┐
│            Controls             │
└─────────────────────────────────┘
┌─────────────────────────────────┐
│       Business process          │
│        transactions             │
└─────────────────────────────────┘
```

Figure 31

This automation comes in three layers:

1. At the base is continuous monitoring of transactions. This analysis is of the quality of the transaction process—correct inputs (including checks *within* the process), process and outputs to a time specification (such as low-latency trading). The point is that software is monitoring the transaction to fix the individual transaction and prevent a problem from cascading.

2. The next layer up is the controls. Here, a software tool looks at the *assurance* controls layered over the processes to see what is being detected and/or corrected. This data is used to both flag errors in a compliance sense and—importantly—to quantify improvement by understanding where problems are causing rework cost, delays and/or lost revenue.

3. The top layer is the audit. This can be for either the testing of the controls or the underlying transaction. Audits should provide risk-based assurance. Adding automation is a way to efficiently improve focus on higher risk areas.

The important point is that each layer can build on those below it, taking advantage of automation in the lower layers to reduce the cost of its own activity. This helps an operational risk manager in at least two ways. First, it points ownership toward the core process in the bottom layer and the business leader responsible. This is the person who has the 'big picture' process perspective and who can make the decision to improve core process as opposed to layering on controls. Second, it points to making a better business case for automation if the stakeholders at each layer (business process, quality improvement, process improvement, risk management, internal control and audit) cooperate in sharing in the costs and benefits. Today, funds are too often wasted (and sometimes redundant tools purchased) when stakeholders miss the common benefit from a shared monitoring tool.

Guidance on this topic has been published: See COSO, The Institute of Internal Auditors and ISACA. A helpful article with a focus on operations improvement is 'Internal Audit's Role in Continuous Monitoring', written by Michael Cangemi and published in the April 2010 issue of The EDP Audit, Control and Security (EDPACS) Newsletter. Mr Cangemi is a former Chief Audit Executive and Chief Financial Officer, and member of the COSO Board.[31]

Optimizing controls—the harmful and the helpful

Harmful

Some organizations seek to 'simplify' their controls by merely reducing the number of their controls. Sometimes this is done by rolling up controls; sometimes it is done by a test of significance. Both have limitations.

The first method risks losing timely insights into problems and allowing cascades to roll on, increasing damage.

The second approach might provide a reasonable sorting of controls, but *only if* significance is judged on more than the individual control. To be effective, it would have to look at the impact of unfolding events both prior to and after the control. If it doesn't, it will miss the full impact of a cascade through the system. For example, think of an individual control in a fraud, industrial accident or the sub-prime mess. It is difficult to find the one control in advance that will have *both* predictive insight *and* be close enough to root

---

[31] COSO (January 2009). 'Guidance on Monitoring Internal Control Systems'.

The Institute of Internal Auditors, Altamonte Springs. (2005), 'Continuous Auditing: Implications for Assurance, Monitoring, and Risk Assessment', Global Technology Audit Guide Series.

ISACA, Rolling Meadows (2010). 'Monitoring Internal Control Systems and IT: A Primer for Business Executives, Managers and Auditors on How to Embrace and Advance Best Practices'.

Cangemi, Michael. (April 2010), 'Internal Audit's Role in Continuous Monitoring', *The EDP Audit, Control and Security Newsletter*, (Taylor & Francis).

cause. Thus, in practice, neither of the two approaches is acceptable for controls that are expected to intercept problems early, be as close to root cause as possible, and prevent or reduce the magnitude of loss. What's an operational risk manager to do?

Helpful

Instead of cutting the number of controls—along with early warning, and ability to prevent and reduce—**a better approach is to simplify by standardizing the design and implementation of controls**. Just like the effect of standardizing light controls (light switches) in your house to a few types, standardizing business controls makes them easier to implement, test and use by a broader range of people and more quickly.

Once standardized, look for 'natural' control points to insert them into business processes. This is made easier by using business process flow diagrams, software-use diagrams and related process maps that were brought into your scenario-analysis workshops.

The savings in design, implementation and testing could even be used to deploy more controls to better prevent and/or reduce impact. Across industries and disciplines, this is a proven approach to making risk management more efficient and effective. The examples cited from hospitals, electric power, chemical and petroleum, and transportation all apply here. Or, walk over to your trading floor and ask a trader (or market risk manager) why standardized information on trading screens is valuable.

To be meaningful, controls must provide insight for action if a threshold is breached. Would you want the next airplane you fly in to be equipped with only the simple 'check engine' light that's on your car dashboard? Get the detail needed to focus action.

The operational risk leader difference

Manage options

Understand the business value of your options to act, the value of knowing now, rather than later, the value of acting now, rather than later—having *more time to act*; and the value of having several response options, rather than being forced into one.

Find balance

Ensure a balance:

- between controls and process improvement so as to mitigate events cascading into greater losses

- in the number, placement and design of controls to balance efficiency and effectiveness

- testing by both managerial and audit roles.

Create levers

Controls can both be part of a business process and can monitor it (without changing it). Whether part of the process or monitoring, controls strengthen the capability to protect against bad things and take advantage of good things.

Design solutions

Control design is a team sport, where participation from risk management, internal control, internal audit, quality control, operations management, business line, functional area, regions, business-process improvement, application design and other teams can significantly improve efficiency and effectiveness. Bring these people together to help risk owners implement better solutions. Leverage the output of scenario-analysis workshops.

Key points

- A control measures conformance with specification and acts on that information.

- The cost/benefit of a control depends heavily on how it is designed into a business-process flow.

- The cost/benefit of a control structure can be improved with continuous monitoring and by simplifying the design of controls.

2.5. Improving Product Management and Fraud Prevention

"It's important to understand how a product works to prevent operational losses. For example, in a community bank (or indeed any other bank), consider a credit product and the potential for operational losses from fraud. The best example that comes to mind is in the bond portfolio if banks accept certain incremental risk exposures in exchange for slightly higher yields. For instance, in the late 1990s many debt instruments were issued with 'credit enhancement' features that allowed them to be traded at slightly higher yields. The credit enhancement features seemed relatively benign, until the market turned and bankers were required to recognize significant losses on assets that they believed to be largely risk free. A root-cause analysis of product would have required a more thorough understanding of the risks associated with that investment instrument and that instrument probably would have been rejected for being inconsistent with the investment parameters of the bank. Variations on this long-standing problem continue today."

— *Mark Olson*

"When I was at Chase, we had significant focus on reducing risk in products, sadly because of several losses. This taught us to get to the product process details. For example, I once ran a business line responsible for letters of credit. Part of the process was a unit of 20 bicycle messengers. In one situation, a perfume manufacturer imported perfume essence in drums from France. The drums would not be released by the shipping company until documents

were presented to demonstrate that payment had been made to the French seller.

"Now I would see the chits from the bicycle messengers stamped 'will call'. I asked the chief messenger what this meant. He said it meant 'the customer will call us when they are willing to pay us'. So, the bicycle messenger became a loan officer! You have got to do the food-chain analysis to get to the details of the process. This was an operational risk that cascaded into a credit risk. Risks can be reduced by understanding how the product process actually works to prevent frauds and mistakes. To understand the risks of existing products, walk through something like a credit card transaction in detail. Big product changes should come to the board. For example, if a bank has an agreement with MasterCard and then they want to add Visa. In general, a CEO should come to the board and say here is a big new product, the risks, why and what is being done to manage risk."

— **Marsh Carter**

Product management and fraud

Product management matters to risk to operations. **Product management creates the products that are sold to generate profitable revenue**. These products are conceived, developed, marketed, sold, delivered and supported in the core business product cycle that was mentioned earlier.

Weaknesses in product management can lead to at least three types of harm to business performance:

1. lost revenue or cost due to time delay and other inefficiencies in the product process itself (program management risk)

2. lost revenue or cost due to product design risk

3. lost revenue or cost due to daily sales and delivery risk (especially from poorly designed products with more risk).

In a financial institution, with its complex systems and operations, these weaknesses lead to specific damage to performance. For example: being late to market; not responding to customer needs in key market segments (under-banked consumers, high-value individuals, or mid-market treasury services); and errors in key offerings (mobile banking and fee-generating products). These can be big problems in a tough economy and in view of recent regulatory changes.

Note: These revenue decreases are losses to shareholders and debt holders, but are not usually 'losses' for regulatory reporting purposes.

In addition to lost revenue, weaknesses in product design cause reportable losses in the clients, products and business practices; fraud; and execution, delivery and process management categories (where IT gaps also are a root-cause factor) of the Basel accords.

In the 2008 Loss Data Collection Exercise, these data points stand out:

- clients, products and business practices
    - corporate finance 47.0% of total losses
    - retail brokerage 66.9%
- external fraud
    - retail banking 40.3%
    - commercial banking 26.5%
    - payment and settlement 25.6%.

As has been cautioned previously; the 2008 numbers are a point in time based on the quality of methods at that time; and they do not include revenue losses. In addition, there is a concern about regulatory penalties under market conduct regulations due to weaknesses in product design, sales or delivery.[32]

Frauds

Frauds deserve extra attention here for at least four reasons.

First, because of their prominence among total losses.

Second, because they are a good example of the earlier discussion on cascading events and loss impacts. Cascades beyond the institution include costs of investigation and prosecution, and to guarantee funds.

Third, because anti-fraud efforts are an example of where improved business processes are viewed as reducing the cost of fraud fighting. For example, the US Federal Bureau of Investigation's (FBIs) *Financial Crimes Section Report*

---

[32] Table IDL 4A Results from the '2008 Loss Collection Exercise for Operational Risk', Basel Committee on Banking Supervision, Bank for International Settlements (July 2009).

to the Public for Fiscal Year 2009 cites the Electronic Bank Record Initiative (EBRI) with the expectation that it will "greatly increase the efficiency of the financial records production process and provide significant cost savings to both the government and private industry."

Fourth, because these are criminal actions consuming time and resources (including damage to reputation) beyond simply 'taking the loss.'

In the US, the Federal Bureau of Investigation's financial crimes section categorizes crimes as:

- corporate fraud
- securities and commodities fraud
- health care fraud
- mortgage fraud
- insurance fraud
- mass marketing fraud
- money laundering.[33]

Each category of fraud intersects with a financial institution in a different way. Abbreviating much, it is helpful to look at some of the investigation categories used by the FBI in more detail.

Corporate fraud

- Falsification of financial information:
    - false accounting entries
    - bogus trades designed to inflate profit or hide losses
    - false transactions designed to evade regulatory oversight.
- Self-dealing by corporate insiders:
    - insider trading
    - kickbacks

---

[33] 'Financial Crimes Report to the Public Fiscal Year 2009', Federal Bureau of Investigation, United States Government.

- backdating of executive stock options
- misuse of corporate property for personal gain
- individual tax violations related to self-dealing.

- Obstruction of justice designed to conceal any of the above-noted types of criminal conduct.

Securities and commodities fraud

- Market manipulation (creating artificial buying pressure for a targeted security)
- high-yield investment fraud (offers of low- or no-risk investments that guarantee unusually high rates of return, including Ponzi, pyramid, and prime bank schemes [victims offered instruments from allegedly preferred sources])
- advance fee fraud
- hedge fund fraud (a range of frauds in a hedge fund setting)
- commodities fraud (false or deceptive sales practices)
- foreign exchange fraud (false or deceptive sales practices)
- broker embezzlement (often through forged documentation or unauthorized trading)
- late-day trading.

Mortgage fraud

- Inflated appraisals
- fictitious/stolen identities
- nominee/straw buyers
- false loan applications
- fraudulent supporting loan documentation
- kickbacks.

Insurance fraud

- Insurance-related corporate fraud

- premium diversion/unauthorized entities (by agents and brokers for their own benefit)

- viatical settlement fraud (a viatical settlement is a discounted, pre-death sale of an existing life insurance policy on the life of a person known to have a terminal condition. This fraud category includes both misrepresentation made on policy applications and, by sellers, misleading benefits expectations)

- workers' compensation fraud (selling unauthorized and non-admitted workers' compensation coverage to businesses)

- disaster fraud (includes false solicitation of charitable contributions, claims fraud by insurers and frauds by contractors)

- staged auto accidents.

Money laundering is a significant concern to financial institutions, and can be thought of as an exploitation of a financial institution's transaction processing systems. This is of particular concern in areas of the world where other systems (such as third-party money transfer, especially mobile-phone-based) can insert high numbers of transactions into financial institution systems.

In reviewing this list, it becomes clear that many frauds are simply an exploited weakness in a product process. If there were no gaps in design, sales or delivery, there would be fewer frauds. And fewer problems in other areas, such as know your customer. (A plaintiff can always sue, but it's much more difficult to win a case when the defendant has solid product processes.)

The Association of Certified Fraud Executives (ACFE) reports that the most frequent method for initial detection of fraud is a tip line. Tips in non-profits, public companies and governments detect over 40% of frauds. A variety of reviews and audits find others. About 10% are not found until by accident, confession or when police notify the company.[34] The frauds in this report are cross-industry composition, not exactly like those in financial institutions.

---

[34] Association of Certified Fraud Executives. (2010),'Report to the Nations on Occupational Fraud and Abuse', (Austin, Texas), p.19.

Still, it tends to reinforce the FBI data and suggests room for improvement in fraud detection and the need for a new tool, such as product management discipline, in the anti-fraud toolbox.

Therefore, to protect revenue generation and avoid loss, engaging the product management discipline is a top opportunity for risk managers seeking to reduce risk to operations. This is especially important when the business case for risk reduction/process improvement can include the reduction in fraud losses, reduction in inefficiencies and, in some situations, increased revenue from more quickly designed, changed or released products. The efficiency point has double value because this approach to finding frauds also expands the benefit of the time and effort spent in product management.

From a regulatory perspective, the Committee of European Banking Supervisors (CEBS) has also recognized this important aspect of new product management. Principle 20—New Products states: "An institution should have in place a well-documented new product approval policy ('NPAP'), approved by the management body, which addresses the development of new markets, products and services and significant changes to existing ones." CEBS connects this back to scenario analysis in Paragraph 115 where they state: "… its input should include a full and objective assessment of risks arising from new activities under a variety of scenarios, of any potential shortcomings in the institution's risk management and internal control frameworks, and of the ability of the institution to manage any new risks effectively."[35]

Regulators are also concerned about the impact of product design considerations as it relates to market conduct questions. This has long been a high-profile consideration in insurance. In banking and financial markets, product design issues are receiving more consideration through the US Dodd-Frank Act's provisions regarding consumer protection, the EU's review of provisions of the Markets in Financial Instruments Directive and the UK Financial Services Authority's expanded focus on Product Intervention.[36] A more risk aware product management process can be used to more cost-effectively address both performance and compliance concerns.

---

[35] CEBS (October 13 2010), 'Consultation paper on the Guidebook on Internal Governance (CP 44)'.

[36] Financial Services Authority. (2011), *Product Intervention*, Discussion Paper 11/1 (DP11/1).

Product management team, process and techniques

The importance of product management should be readily apparent to us as consumers of financial products—How easily does the new mobile application work? Can funds really be transferred between any two accounts? Do banking products fully integrate with business and consumer financial management software? Who designed that sub-prime mortgage approval process? How could 'robo-signings' of home foreclosure documentation have happened?

To bring the benefits of each type of reduced risk in product management to the institution, the operational risk manager needs to *know the business* regarding product management. Product management processes vary across institutions due to factors such as size, business lines, product lines and organizational design. Yet all product management processes share common elements from a common body of professional knowledge across industries. A gold standard in the field of product management is *New Products Management*, Ninth Edition, by Merle Crawford and Anthony Di Benedetto (McGraw-Hill Irwin, 2008).

Drawing on that book, the next section is a brief overview of what an operational risk manager should expect to find in a good product management process. This includes roles involved, phases of product management and techniques most relevant for managing risk.

Team

The typical product management team is led by a product manager. The product manager may report to the business line executive or to a central product management team assigned to a business line. The other members of the product team include representatives of each of the functional areas needed to conceive, design, create, launch, refine and retire the product offering. These representatives include strategy, competitive analysis, market analysis, marketing, operations, IT (often multiple areas such as architecture, applications, infrastructure, security and recovery), business continuity, sales, distribution channel sales (if a product is sold through independent brokers, dealers or agents), legal, finance and human resources. In addition, the team might include an assigned project manager as well as internal advisors from business-process improvement or quality control. Depending on the nature of a product, market or credit risk would be at the table. And, if you are not already there, operational risk.

For the operational risk manager this is an excellent 'meet point' through which to engage the business. Better still, this is engaging around enabling revenue and business performance, not just compliance.

Process and techniques

A typical product-management process consists of five phases: opportunity identification and selection; concept generation; concept/project evaluation; development; and launch. The process can be viewed as iterative, so that post-launch evaluation feeds back into product refinements. These are illustrated in the following diagram.

The basic new products process

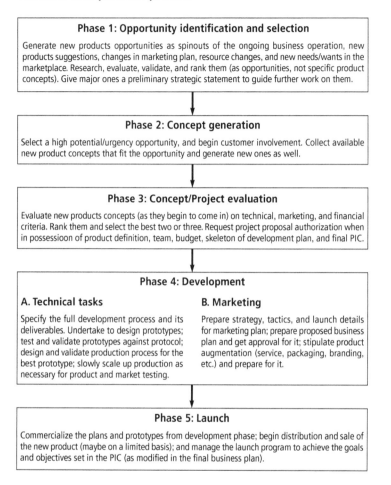

Phase 1: Opportunity identification and selection

Generate new products opportunities as spinouts of the ongoing business operation, new products suggestions, changes in marketing plan, resource changes, and new needs/wants in the marketplace. Research, evaluate, validate, and rank them (as opportunities, not specific product concepts). Give major ones a preliminary strategic statement to guide further work on them.

Phase 2: Concept generation

Select a high potential/urgency opportunity, and begin customer involvement. Collect available new product concepts that fit the opportunity and generate new ones as well.

Phase 3: Concept/Project evaluation

Evaluate new products concepts (as they begin to come in) on technical, marketing, and financial criteria. Rank them and select the best two or three. Request project proposal authorization when in possessioon of product definition, team, budget, skeleton of development plan, and final PIC.

Phase 4: Development

A. Technical tasks

Specify the full development process and its deliverables. Undertake to design prototypes; test and validate prototypes against protocol; design and validate production process for the best prototype; slowly scale up production as necessary for product and market testing.

B. Marketing

Prepare strategy, tactics, and launch details for marketing plan; prepare proposed business plan and get approval for it; stipulate product augmentation (service, packaging, branding, etc.) and prepare for it.

Phase 5: Launch

Commercialize the plans and prototypes from development phase; begin distribution and sale of the new product (maybe on a limited basis); and manage the launch program to achieve the goals and objectives set in the PIC (as modified in the final business plan).

Figure 32

Figure from *New Products Management*, Ninth Edition, by Merle Crawford and Anthony Di Benedetto (McGraw-Hill Irwin, 2008). Used by permission. Copyright © 2008 The McGraw-Hill Companies, Inc.

For products with complex selling processes, a sales process may be added to the product-management process with steps for identifying sales opportunities, evaluating customer needs, tailoring a solution to the customer and closing the sale. This is often the case with corporate finance, private banking or wealth-management offerings as opposed to mass-market retail banking offerings.

Between each phase of the product process, a decision is made to advance the proposed offering to the next step. These steps are sometimes called 'stage gates'. The more costly a product offering is to develop, the more likely it is that stage gates will be added at points where additional resources must be released. The caution in applying stage gates, checkpoints or other methods is to avoid excessive overhead or stifle innovation. As in anything, there is a risk-return balance. As an operational risk manager, you have an opportunity to share a perspective with the team. Examples of evaluation tasks are illustrated in the diagram below.

The evaluation tasks in the new products process

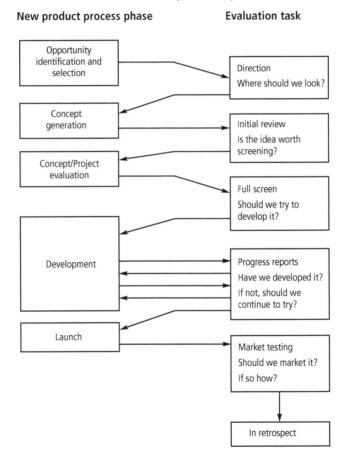

Figure 33

Figure from *New Products Management*, Ninth Edition, by Merle Crawford and Anthony Di Benedetto (McGraw-Hill Irwin, 2008). Used by permission. Copyright © 2008 The McGraw-Hill Companies, Inc.

From the perspective of risk to operations, the risk manager can add an additional set of questions to help the team reflect on risks that must be accepted due to the nature of the product/customer combination and those that can be reduced by adjustments in product features or supporting business-IT processes.

Looking at each phase of the process, example questions include the following.

Opportunity identification and selection

Team operations

Has a project manager been assigned to manage risk within the product team?

Does the team have the appropriate members with knowledge of the various operational areas of an institution in order to develop and launch potential products? Who has been left out? Examples include operational and IT representatives of other business lines that will supply key capabilities, a regional representative concerned with local conditions, and a regulatory affairs person appropriate to new jurisdictions or customer types.

Are opportunity areas aligned with available product platforms (implying lower cost to develop and faster time to market)? For example, one financial institution had three retail banking platforms from three acquisitions. One was initially chosen based on feature/function strength, but later had problems scaling. It had to be replaced.

Is the team operating with a clear product innovation charter (PIC)? The PIC should include statements on: market situation; business strategy; a technology or market dimension focus (e.g. mobile banking or under-banked consumers); goals and measures; and 'rules of the road' (often guidance from the executive sponsors such as support for multiple languages in the target market; cross-sell packaging for wealth-management products; requirements for agent channel distribution; or compliance sensitivities).

Concept generation

Is the product concept worth pursuing? At this stage, the team has generated a range of potential product concepts to pursue. The evaluation task is to narrow that list down to those with the most revenue potential and the least cost and risk (both in implementation and market). This is a rough analysis before moving the concept to the next phase for more serious evaluation.

When considering risks from operations to the success of a product, the value of a risk manager is to raise early potential risks for the team. Part of this depends on ensuring the right subject matter experts are at the table to share their insights. Understanding can also then come from sharing risk analyses of similar products to put risks of the new product in perspective. Often a team will be aware of a general problem, but the magnitude or likelihood of the problem is not clear. These are benefits of risk management involvement, but they are only protecting against loss; they are not enabling revenue.

A way for the risk manager to bring more value to the discussion is to share analysis on how problems were overcome in other situations. For example, an alternative product technology platform and business process was used elsewhere that reduced risk to product success. Or, the risk manager can improve communications. For example, strategy and regulatory leaders are considering an exit from certain markets due to excessive business risk. If so, the risk leader can share this information so the team can screen out concepts with this excessive risk.

At this point of rough-cut analysis, the objective is to ensure that the team has a solid grounding in the environment and enterprise-capability risk evaluation so they can filter concepts most appropriately.

Concept/Project evaluation

At this stage a few (maybe only one) product concept is being considered. Key questions include:

- What is the likelihood this product concept will be successful given our enterprise operational requirements?

- What changes will have to be made to reduce the risk to success?

- What is the risk of making those changes? After that is done, what risk will remain to the product's success?

Again, the risk manager relies on cross-silo analysis and bringing the appropriate people to the table to help the team answer these questions.

Two tools are particularly helpful in understanding risk to operations (and strategy):

1. The A-T-A-R analysis approach refers to awareness, trial, availability and repeat. It asks how likely it is that a number of prospective customers will be aware off the product offering; will try it; will be able to easily access

it through a distribution channel (mobile, web, branch, agent/broker); and then will purchase it again. The actual logic varies by product/consumer type. For example, some consumers are quicker than others to change checking accounts; property and casualty insurance is switched more frequently than life insurance; some investment customers consolidate accounts at a single broker, others have multiple.

2. The product protocol is also known as 'product definition' or 'product requirements'. It describes the product concept in several ways. These include: target market and positioning; specific attributes (features and functions, including ease-of-use in web applications); competitive concerns; cross-sell expectations; marketing and sales channel needs; financial expectations; operational requirements (such as systems availability to download transactions and data location needs); legal and regulatory considerations (both solvency and market conduct, such as data privacy requirements and know your customer); and other risks in development, implementation and delivery.

The risk manager can use both of these tools and others to help the team answer the key operational questions. **The risk manager's value contribution comes from helping the team consider these risks early and bringing together the right knowledge to reduce risk**. For example, have the technology-architecture and business process improvement teams been cooperating on a project to improve business processes on which this new offering depends? If so, bring them to the table. This could reduce risk and cost to a new offering.

Development

At this stage, a product concept has been approved and it is moving into development. Three aspects of the development process are relevant to the operational risk manager:

1. That the right team was assembled to reflect the range of identified risks and the ways to respond to them.

2. That a product-use test was conducted that carefully considered risks, including gaps that could be exploited for fraud, market-conduct compliance (including the home foreclosure robo-signing problem) or solvency implications. The product-use test is a form of scenario analysis described earlier. To make this test easier, the modified or new product can simply be placed in the context of an existing scenario, describing

what could threaten the process and how it could break. The software application development team is a helpful ally here, as they have expertise in testing various 'use case' scenarios against the application design to see what might cause an error condition in the application, or other problems such as vulnerability to fraud.

3. Controls are built in to the product processes. Development should also include preparedness measures and early warning indicators to reflect any new characteristics of the product, customer set or jurisdiction. The more the new product/customer/market/jurisdiction combination is different from existing products, the more that extra controls and early warning indicators might be appropriate until the product is considered stabilized. Remember, organizational and core product maturity can be traded off against controls. The more solid the organization and core product processes, the less controls are needed. Thus, controls on something new or changed can be tapered over time to find the right cost/benefit.

The risk manager must probe each area. The first and third points have been addressed already. The new consideration here is the product-use test. These product-use tests can be more or less formal. To best help anticipate and reduce risk to operations, two suggestions are offered:

- Consider the sales and delivery process in light of scenarios developed earlier in the seek scenarios section. Does the new product trigger any of the event flows illustrated in the scenarios? If so, act to address them now.

- Second, **conduct a live walkthrough of the product with as much realism as possible**. As pointed out by our board member viewpoints—and as we shall see in an extended conversation with them all later in this book—this is key. For example, consider the sales training that would be offered with the product launch. Practice that now within the team. To avoid bias, test with people who have not been part of the team and are thus less likely to assume the correct answer. If the offering involves a software application for customers or employees, the development team will likely have a mock-up or prototype. Test it thoroughly (again, with people from outside the team) to see if it triggers risks to operations, and find ways to fix those. **Look for those gaps that could be exploited for fraud, waste, market conduct or other operational problems**. Finally, continue this walkthrough of any new IT management processes, looking for similar gaps that could threaten operational stability, availability, protection or recoverability. For example, 'new' processes are often set up in smaller, more flexible data centers. This is good for speed, but those smaller centers might also be less protected and recoverable.

Launch

For the launch phase, the risk manager is in a role similar to that of a market risk manager or space flight controller—watching for early warnings and being prepared to help the team act as the launch unfolds.

Depending on the institution and scope of the risk manager, this risk monitoring may or may not include risks to sales revenue, and the budget and timeline of the product team.

Depending on the risk (either market or technology) in the new offering, the launch may follow a limited roll-out plan in certain geographic regions or customer types. Such precautions can help 'shake out' product, business process and technology process weaknesses before they experience the full volume of transactions.

> **Tip**: In risk reporting, the information flow might follow a dual path. One path that is integrated with the product team to the sponsoring executives; the second path through risk management channels. To save costs in reporting, consider audiences in advance and combine data-gathering efforts. For example, special reporting may be required on market conduct issues for the jurisdictions involved.

The product-management discipline offers a large body of knowledge to the financial institution, including books such as Crawford and DiBenetto recommended here and the publications and education from the Product Development and Management Association (**www.pdma.org**). **You can use this body of knowledge to: a) better evaluate risk in products and process, and b) help product-management teams accelerate risk response to reduce loss and improve revenue opportunities. In short, to improve business performance within the system of a product, and its customers, competitors and malicious threats**.

Key points

- Product management creates the products that are sold to generate profitable revenue.

- Many frauds are simply an exploited weakness in a product process.

- The risk manager's value contribution comes from helping the team consider these risks early and bringing together the right knowledge to reduce risk.

2.6. Improving IT-related Business Risk Management

"Product processes are increasingly implemented through information technology, so there is increased risk of failure and greater need to find root cause. This includes both complete failures in systems and performance problems such as increased transaction latency that can cause loss because trades are not completed at the best price. We have seen significant failures in financial institution IT systems. This reminds us that we just need to keep pushing our dependency analyses to see what problems can arise and how technology can help us (such as transaction monitoring to better check for errors). We also need to stay disciplined on preventative measures such as parallel systems before fully switching to the new system."

— *Marsh Carter*

"In the case of IT-related operational risk, we look at the details that matter to our customers and regulators. For example, we hire 'white hat' (good guy) hackers to conduct penetration testing on our network. In the wire room, we review approval procedures to avoid fraud in outgoing wire transfers. In addition, we look at how we can use analytics to more quickly and clearly evaluate risks to our banking operations."

— *Humphrey Polanen*

Financial services depend on information technology

Financial institutions of all sizes are becoming more and more dependent on IT systems to deliver business performance outcomes. The chapters on dependency mapping and scenario analysis have already raised this ever-growing dependency. Consider entire stock exchanges, where previously humans engaged in open outcry trading, that are now just a 'box in a basement'. Online banking and mobile banking are entirely IT dependent. Even The so-called branch of the future is highly automated, reserving human interaction for sales activity and personalized customer service. Insurance carrier relationships with agents and competitive advantage are highly dependent on ease of use and quality of information provided through information systems.

At a conference, several risk managers were enjoying lunch. One told a story of a small fire in a seemingly insignificant data center in New England. The fire stopped operations in the center, but as a small and old center there was no further concern. But soon, she began to receive phone calls from across the company telling of critical systems outages. No one really knew what business processes actually depended on that 'insignificant' center! To a person, each of us around the table had a similar story.

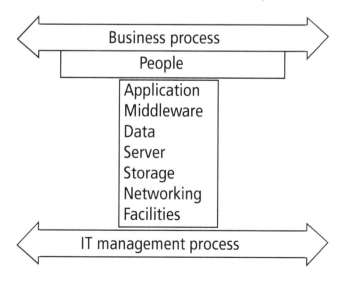

Figure 34

In risk management, there are three interactions with IT. First, technology operations and components can suffer problems that cause loss in business activities, products and processes that depend on IT. Second, technology can reduce risk in business activities, products and processes by bringing new efficiency and effectiveness through automation and integration. Third, technology can improve risk management through improved information collection, analysis, presentation and tracking.

Humphrey Polanen is particularly emphatic on this third use of technology to improve risk management:

> "It's vital to be more predictive with early warnings. In my experience, in both the computer industry and banking we are continually surprised by how quickly things can deteriorate. We wish we could have acted earlier to find the root cause of problems and avoid them. We need end-to-end visibility in our operational systems. For example, credit risk is out there all the time. The question is how quickly we can see a credit (or market) problem and react to it. That visibility comes through operational systems and the analytics to turn data points into early warnings. Data that gets to the risk management steering committee or the board 30 to 60 days after the fact is not an early warning. So data is the biggest impediment to better risk management on an operational level. This can be addressed through improved core systems (where asset values are recorded) and then in the risk management systems and dashboards."

IT and risk management

For the operational risk leader, the managerial needs are to:

1. ensure that management of IT-related business risk connects to the operational risk management function of the institution (in terms of organizational structures, processes and communication)

2. ensure that the IT-related business risk management function is doing its job of bringing together all of the individual silos of IT-related business risk. These silos include: IT investment portfolio management (that is also tied to strategic risk); business-IT program/project management; and then the silos in the IT operations/service delivery (e.g. application development; change; availability; perimeter and data security; back-up/recovery; facilities; and energy).

The operational risk management leader needs confidence that a risk management process is in place to manage this myriad of risks on which the revenue-generation capability of the institution is dependent.

Further, these IT-related business risks must be evaluated, reported and managed in a way that is explicitly tied to a business unit, line, product or other activity. A business unit leader should not be subjected to a parade of risk managers saying, "Here are your problems, fix them" with no context on how they relate to the business or priorities to address. For example, is the gap in change management, project management or availability management more urgent to address?

Problems in information systems damage business performance and receive regulatory attention.

After the March 2011 Japan earthquake, Mizuho bank suffered a cascading systems failure. According to a 31 May 2011 independent review committee report, a large volume of transactions related to the earthquake combined with outdated systems, led to a batch job failure. This triggered a chain of events compounded by errors in manual responses. This included the ATM network failure, especially troubling during the post-earthquake need for cash. The failures also complicated fiscal year-end closings. Among the causal factors identified were weaknesses in risk evaluation in general (scenario analysis in particular), risk evaluation of new products, crisis management and training..

From the UK Financial Services Authority (FSA):

> "*August 25, 2010*: The Financial Services Authority (FSA) has fined the London branch of Société Générale (SocGen) £1,575,000 for failing to provide accurate transaction reports to the FSA. The fine reflects the seriousness of SocGen's failure to submit accurate reports for approximately 80% of its reportable transactions, across all of its asset classes, for a period of over two years."[37]

> "*August 24, 2010*: The Financial Services Authority (FSA) has fined the UK branch of Zurich Insurance Plc (Zurich UK) £2,275,000 for failing to have adequate systems and controls in place to prevent the loss of customers' confidential information. The fine is the highest levied to date on a single firm for data security failings."[38]

---

[37] www.fsa.gov.uk/pubs/final/societe_generale.pdf.

[38] www.fsa.gov.uk/pubs/final/zuric_plc.pdf.

From the Monetary Authority of Singapore (MAS):

"*August 4, 2010*: MAS censured DBS Bank for the shortcomings and inadequate management oversight by the bank of its outsourced IT systems, networks, operations and infrastructure that resulted in the widespread system outage on 5 July 2010. This incident revealed weaknesses in DBS Bank's technology and operational risk management controls. MAS has required DBS Bank to apply a multiplier of 1.2 times to its risk-weighted assets for operational risk, which translates to the bank setting aside an additional amount of approximately SGD 230 million (about USD 170 million) in regulatory capital on a group basis based on numbers as of 30 June 2010. The additional capital requirement will be reviewed when MAS is satisfied that the bank has put in place adequate risk control measures to address the deficiencies identified. The additional capital requirement would take DBS to Tier 1 capital of about 13% and total capital at risk to just over 16%."[39]

CAUTION: When reviewing news stories like these and others, operational risk leaders are warned to remember the method used in Basel-based compliance reporting. With reporting on a proximate-cause basis, many losses that are root-cause-based in information systems are reported in other categories. Consider events from rogue trading to the sub-prime mess, where improved IT systems or management thereof (such as access controls) could have prevented, improved detection or reduced the severity of an adverse event. When considering losses that could have been *prevented* by IT-related measures, the percentage of IT-related losses grows even higher.

---

[39] **bit.ly/ciVJXt.**

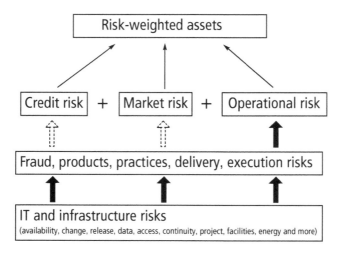

Figure 35 [And with thanks to Gabriel David.]

Thus, IT-related operational risk on a root-cause basis is larger than would appear in the business disruption and system failure category reports.

Good institutions, performing scenario and root-cause analysis, seek ways to better spotlight IT-related business risks. Knowing this, a simple and helpful tool is change analysis. In particular, track **the magnitude and speed of change**. When this is done, root causes seem to fall into some relatively actionable categories:[40]

Significant business change

- Environment: competitors, market, regulation, social.

- Management: organization design, executive change.

- Activity: acquisition, consolidation, expansion, new product, new jurisdiction.

---

[40] List used by permission of ValueBridge Advisors, LLC.

For example, poor integration after mergers and acquisitions can be particularly vexing. Not just at the infrastructure level, but also in operational performance of customer-facing or internal financial systems (are transactions being recorded properly?). Often the 'simple' solution—to keep both systems running in parallel—becomes complex in daily operations.

Significant technology change

Environment: competitors, market, regulation, social.

Management: cost take-out, shared services, data center consolidation or 'green' environmental initiatives.

For example, pure complexity of the IT environment has been illustrated as a significant factor in increasing risk. For an excellent discussion of this, please see chapter 2 of the book *IT Risk: Turning Business Threats into Competitive Advantage* by George Westerman and Richard Hunter.[41]

Inappropriate use of cost-reduction approaches (such as 'Lean') increase risk when they are applied with an approach that says: 'Withdraw resources until something breaks, then stop, pause, and try again.' This find-the-limit-by-failure approach endangers operational performance.

The rubber-band and chewing-gum method of management is a variation of inappropriate cost reduction. When multiple components are each running in the danger zone, the risk of system failure rockets up (for more, please see the section on factor analysis). This is worse when each individual knows how at-risk their IT components are, but is not fully aware of the risk taken by others, and increases risk when they push even further into risky territory assuming they can fall back on others.

Failure to properly align business and IT objectives, including willingness to take risk. In some cases, business leaders are happily ignorant of the IT-related risk to their business objectives. In other cases, business leaders (and members of boards of directors) want to fully understand the risk, yet IT managers wrongly assume that those leaders don't care or would just push for more cost reductions. While it might sound so obvious, the value of a fact-based, scenario-based dialogue is difficult to overstate.

---

[41] Westerman, George, and Hunter, Richard. (2007), *IT Risk: Turning Business Threats into Competitive Advantage*. (Cambridge: Harvard Business Press).

Outsourcing, like anything, comes with benefits and risks. Typical outsourcing-related sources of risk are:

1. Priorities get disconnected between the ultimate business client, retained IT management, service-provider IT management and service provider operational personnel.

2. Insufficient evaluation of vendor capability for process and systems monitoring (too often it is only outcomes that are evaluated, missing the leading indicator of capability).

3. Breaking agile development (and other best practices) when functions are split between institution and service provider.

More information on improved evaluation is below.

Platform: virtualization, cloud, mobile/collaboration/web 2.0 or services-oriented architecture.

For example, adding or changing technologies at too quick a pace or without sufficient understanding drives risk. Similarly, removing people who are living histories of technologies currently in place is a recipe for problems.

To visualize these changes, plot them on a 'change chart' graph with magnitude and speed as the axes. Change types can be color-coded. Bubble size can reflect potential impact. The bubbles are examples only for illustration. Change analysis can be easily used to strengthen other business analysis. For example, if several projects are being considered for funding, a change risk indicator can be added as a row in a spreadsheet. To provide more insight in projects, the change indicator can be applied to the design, implementation and operational phases of a project or environmental change (e.g. new regulation).

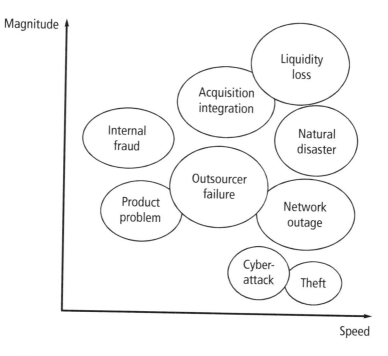

Figure 36

What does the operational risk leader need to know?

The operational risk leader must know to work with the chief information officer (CIO) to build a business-activity-based view of IT-related risk to operations. This is similar to a manufacturing plant final-assembly manager looking back through the entire assembly line to see any risk from suppliers, product, equipment, people, process, facilities and such to successfully completing a product and shipping it out the door.

A 'business activity' can be a business unit, process, line, product or other scope of analysis. To achieve this, a key hurdle (as mentioned earlier) is to cross the range of silos of IT operations.

In building this view, the operational risk leader can reach out to colleagues in business process improvement, quality control, project management, and business continuity with similar objectives to evaluate and improve business-IT processes.

From a resource perspective, the operational risk leader will have an IT-related risk manager. This person will likely dotted-line report to the CIO. In some organizations the IT-related risk manager solid-line reports to the CIO. However, solid line to the operational risk leader provides more independence, especially in light of recent financial services statutory and regulatory changes.

While this is simple in concept, in the past it has been challenging because of the complexity of the financial institution (with diverse business units and geographic regions), the range of IT areas (too often functioning in their own silos), and differing (yet well-developed) risk management terminology and process guidance for each of those IT areas (e.g. finance, project management, operations, security, application development, and continuity).

The task became much simpler when ISACA released *Risk IT Based on COBIT* in 2009. The *Risk IT Essentials, Framework and Practitioner Guide* represented a substantial build-out of the IT-related business risk management content in COBIT 4.1 (released in 2007, COBIT was first released in 1998, and COBIT 5 at the time of writing is coming soon). COBIT covers four areas of IT management: planning and organizing; acquiring and implementing solutions; delivering and support; and monitoring and evaluating.

ISACA, with its 95,000 members in 160 countries, is the primary knowledge-creation organization for the IT oversight, management and assurance disciplines. ISACA's frameworks are available in several languages for global use. *Risk IT* was created based on the requests of practitioners who were struggling with the need to cross the silos within IT and then connect upwards to enterprise-wide risk management. During the course of development, nearly 1900 comments were received from reviewers in about 20 countries. It is the only guidance of its type.

Risk IT has several benefits for operational risk leaders in financial services:

- It embodies the long COBIT history of focus on business goals and objectives.

- With its open availability and long history, it is recommended or required for use by regulators in many countries.

- ISACA provides two specific guidance documents for financial services: *Control Objectives for Basel II* and *Mapping of FFIEC with COBIT 4.1*.

While *Risk IT* is a cross-industry document, it is readily adaptable to financial services organizations. Several of the members of the core team that created *Risk IT* (including your author here) came to the team with financial services experience. Financial services professionals are also a large portion of the ISACA user community.

For example, the generic view of risk categories used in *Risk IT* should be very familiar to a bank.

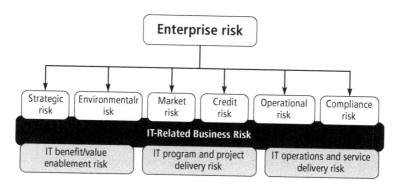

Figure 37 [Source: The Risk IT Framework. © 2009 ISACA. All rights reserved. Used by permission.]

With a few edits in the middle line, an insurer can substitute in 'underwriting risk', 'claims risk', and 'investment risk'. While the phrase 'operational risk' is used by insurers in Europe and other countries, the phrase 'business risk' is more frequently used by insurers in countries such as the US.

Tailoring *Risk IT* to your organization's needs

Risk IT has been mentioned several times in earlier chapters to provide examples of content that are included in a good risk management framework (process flows, maturity models, RACI tables and other tools).

Here, we'll turn to a short tour of the *Risk IT* documentation and tips on how to tailor it to your needs in a financial services organization.

Risk IT, in the spirit of this book, includes several tools. In addition to the process model itself (more about which in a moment), these include:

- tools to aid in scenario analysis (flow diagram and generic scenarios)

- heat maps

- enterprise IT risk assessment form

- example risk impact scales

- risk analysis 'swim lane' chart (roles and flows)

- risk response options and selection parameters

- risk register template

- risk communication flows.

Risk IT is divided into three sections: Essentials, Framework and Practitioner Guide. The first two sections are packaged in one document again entitled (perhaps confusingly) the 'Framework'. Each of the documents is just over 100 pages in length. In addition, ISACA provides a .zip file for download with higher resolution images of some of the key graphics and the key tools provided in .doc and .xls formats to make them easier to customize to your needs.

The Framework

The Framework opens with about 15 pages of introductory and executive summary material. This introduces two key organizing thoughts.

First, the three IT-related risk categories of: **IT Benefit/Value (related to the business-IT investment portfolio); Program/Project Management, and Operations/Service Delivery**. For a bank, most of these three categories are considered operational risk in a Basel II sense (with some strategic risk, too). For an insurer, they would all fall within business risk.

Second, the three domains of: **Risk Governance; Risk Evaluation; and Risk Response**. The Essentials and the Framework itself are organized around these three domains.

Essentials

The document then turns to the Essentials. In 15 pages, it touches on each of the three domains.

- In Risk Governance: Risk Appetite & Tolerance; Responsibilities and Accountability for IT Risk Management; Awareness and Communication;

and Risk Culture. As noted earlier, *Risk IT* includes more guidance on culture than any other risk management framework, standard or best practice.

- In Risk Evaluation: Describing Business Impact and Risk Scenarios. As noted earlier, the *Risk IT* guidance on scenario analysis contains a variety of generic or 'starter' scenarios to stimulate team thinking in creating scenarios for your enterprise.

- In Risk Response: Key Risk Indicators (KRI) and Risk Response Definition and Prioritization. Because of COBIT's long-standing focus on business goals and objectives, KRIs are used to address risk to performance indicators. This section is where the reader is also introduced to *Risk IT*'s emphasis on actually responding to risk, not just evaluating it, to help the risk practitioner deliver value to organizations by solving problems and reducing risk to revenue.

Next is a section on using *Risk IT* in conjunction with ISACA's other two frameworks, COBIT 4.1 and Val IT 2.0. *Risk IT* can be used stand-alone. However, financial services organizations will want to make use of these other frameworks, especially COBIT 4.1, as it is the basis of the Basel II and US FFIEC mapping documents.

Framework

The Framework itself now appears, also based on the three domains of Risk Governance, Risk Evaluation and Risk Response.

Each of these three domains is divided into three processes (and these into sub-processes).

Risk Governance (RG) includes:

- RG1 Establish and maintain a common risk view

- RG2 Integrate with ERM (Enterprise Risk Management)

- RG3 Make risk-aware business decisions

Risk Evaluation (RE) includes:

- RE1 Collect data

- RE2 Analyze risk

- RE3 Maintain risk profile

Risk Response (RR) includes:

- RR1 Articulate risk

- RR2 Manage risk

- RR3 React to events

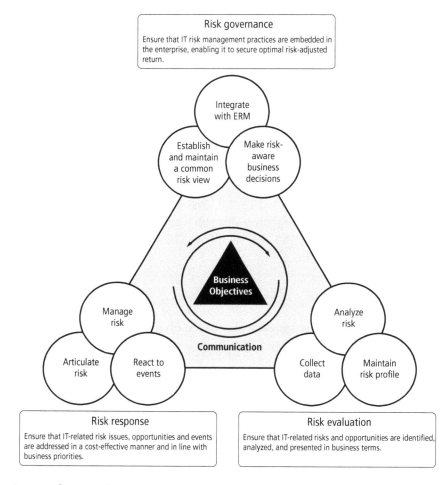

Figure 38 [Source: The Risk IT Framework. © 2009 ISACA. All rights reserved. Used by permission.]

For each domain, a set of standard process elements are covered.

For each domain:

- A graphic overview of the domain within the framework, highlighting the domain goal(s) and metric(s).

- A maturity model in both high-level and detailed views. The detailed model provides 0–5 descriptive ratings on six attributes: awareness and communication; responsibility and accountability; goal setting and measurement; policies, standards and procedures; skills and expertise; tools and automation.

For each process (nine in total, three for each of the three domains):

- Process overview: A graphic overview of the process within the framework, highlighting the process goal and key activities.

- Process detail: Key management practices, with inputs and outputs.

- Management guidelines: RACI charts, goals and metrics.

To adapt the domain and process content to your organization, four primary sets of edits are required:

1. Adjust to your business and IT organizational structure (centralized, federated, decentralized). This has particular impact on the RACI tables and the wording of the maturity model evaluation descriptions.

2. Adjust to your country/industry terminology. If you wish to create separate documentation for each business line, terminology adjustments should be made and emphases should be added.

3. Adjust to your enterprise-wide risk management terminology. To make this easier, in the *Risk IT Practitioner Guide* mappings are provided to the terminology in ISO / IEC Guide 73 (used by FERMA/IRM/ALARM/AIRMIC's (A Risk Management Standard (ARMS) and ISO's 31000) and COSO's Enterprise Risk Management—Integrated Framework).

4. Adjust to your business process for your lines of business and locations. For example, if you offshore all your general ledger operations, what risk do you have of foreign governments seizing all that data and crippling your institution? If you are engaged in trading operations, your risk analysis of availability must consider latency and the ability to support sub-ten-millisecond trading. If you operate in large cities and require

alternative workspace for recovery operations, what happens if multiple customers of your alternative workspace all need that space at once? Who gets the space? If you are involved in settlement, custodial or other operations deemed to be high in systemic risk, is your IT designed to operate at much higher levels of stability and availability? If the financial data you hold (yours or your customers') can be modified in a country outside your home jurisdiction, does your insider-threat management cover more than disgruntled employees or rogue traders—does it also guard against organized crime or government-sponsored espionage? The core material for all these areas can be found in open best practices; you need to tailor in a way that is appropriate to your environment.

As a practical matter, any organization implementing any standard or practice must decide whether to tailor at the central level and distribute to users or provide education at the central level and then have users adapt on the fly and report variations. For a description of one organization's approach, you might wish to read the MetLife *Risk IT* case study at **www.isaca.org/riskit**.

The Framework concludes with an extensive list of references and a glossary. The most current glossary is found at **www.isaca.org/glossary**.

The Practitioner Guide

The Practitioner Guide is the second document. It was created in response to public exposure draft comments asking for more guidance on execution. The Framework can be described as the 'what to do' and the Practitioner Guide the 'how to do it'.

The Practitioner Guide opens with a review of the *Risk IT* process model followed by more detail on how to use *Risk IT* along with COBIT 4.1 and Val IT 2.0.

It then turns to eight 'how-tos' driven by reviewer questions:

1. defining a risk universe and scoping risk management

2. risk appetite and risk tolerance

3. risk awareness, communication and reporting; including key risk indicators, risk profiles, risk aggregation and risk culture

4. expressing and describing risk; including guidance on business context, frequency, impact, using the COBIT business-goals approach, risk maps, risk registers

5. risk scenarios; including capability risk factors and environmental risk factors

6. risk response and prioritization

7. a risk-analysis workflow: 'swim lane' flow chart, including role context

8. mitigation of IT risk using COBIT & Val IT; this table points users to actions to reduce risk found in COBIT and Val IT.

Coming to the end, it includes a section that maps principles, process steps and terminology to other risk management standards and frameworks. This is a key reference.

Where do I start?

Such a wealth of material requires a starting point. When applying any standard or practice, the answer is straightforward—start with your biggest pain. This includes the pain you already know about *and* the pain that might be sneaking up on you (the 'unwatched pot'). This suggests two quick analyses.

- First, compare a list of recent problems (with their root causes) to the *Risk IT* domains and processes. This can be as simple as placing a check mark on the diagram (Figure 38 above) for each problem instance (if you like, weighting by severity). This is a quick indicator of current pain.

- Second, with the team, assess the maturity of risk management capabilities and compare to the desired level in a given period (such as one year out). Bigger gaps point to higher potential pain. These capability assessments are leading indicators that provide a view of what problems might arise in the future.

Both analyses can be done at varying levels of detail and with greater or fewer participants to collect a range of views. It is a scalable approach to give you the level of confidence you prefer. As noted earlier, engaging the right people is key to success.

Users typically take some action in all nine of the processes; the priorities relate more to the depth of action taken in any process (or sub-process/activity).

To probe for problems, a pilot might include a few business areas with significant known problems and a few that appear to have no problems. By looking at a process that appears fine, an organization can learn a) what is working that can be duplicated and/or b) lurking problems that need to be addressed before they erupt.

What can I learn from others' experience?

To help answer this question, a survey research study of 258 business and IT executives from six countries provides valuable insight.[42] This study was conducted jointly by the MIT Sloan Center for Information Systems Research and IBM. The authors, George Westerman and the author of this book, asked a series of questions about IT risk management activities, and then the IT and business outcomes experienced. These activities were placed into three groups:

1. **Risk governance** represents the policies and processes used to spot, prioritize, and identify responses to IT risks. Its definition also embraces much of what is in *Risk IT*'s 'Risk Evaluation and Response'.

2. **IT foundation** refers to the actual IT environment (people, processes, software and hardware).

3. **Risk-aware culture** is being aware of risk, being comfortable talking about it and working together to manage it.

Key findings include:

- Organizations that had balanced maturity in their IT risk actions, meaning higher maturity across all three areas, had significantly better IT and business outcomes. Those outcomes were not just about reducing negative IT incidents. They also included managing costs better, ensuring that current functionality was more fully aligned with business needs, and having more agility to support changes in the business.

- Organizations with balanced maturity reported more favorable perceptions of IT risk management capability than those that did not employ all three disciplines. Just 10% of out-of-balance organizations said that IT risks are effectively managed by their companies, while 72% of organizations with balanced maturity made that claim.

---

[42] Westerman, George, and Barnier, Brian. (2008), 'How Mature is Your IT Risk Management?', *MIT Sloan CISR Research Briefing*, Volume VIII, No. 3C, December 2008. Westerman, George, and Barnier, Brian. (2009), 'IT Risk Management: Balanced Maturity Can Yield Big Results', IBM Whitepaper, February 2009. Westerman, George, and Barnier, Brian. (2010), 'Driving New Value from IT Risk Management,' *ISACA Journal*, January 2010.

- The role of risk governance is different from the other two areas. The other areas, foundation and risk-aware culture, are associated most directly with effective outcomes. Risk governance acts as a facilitating function to make the other two more effective, and addresses objectives and perceptions of stakeholders—what oversight is about. Risk governance also seems to play a stronger role early, being more highly associated with positive outcomes as firms start their journey, and then playing more of a support role as organizations become more mature and the focus is on the more direct business impact of improved IT foundation and risk-aware culture.

Special considerations when working with third-party service providers

In obtaining IT services, there are a variety of ways they can be procured. Services can be provided by the institution itself, by a captive, dedicated IT-services company, by an IT-services company owned in a consortium with other institutions, or by a third-party vendor. There are variations in procurement approaches when the sources of service are divided by business lines, geographic areas or type of service (such as custom applications, standardized services, standardized infrastructures—e.g. storage networks—and support services—e.g. security testing).

Many factors influence sourcing decisions. One of the most significant is the business-IT model that evaluates the extent to which IT is important in an organization (and it is very important in any financial institution) and provides differentiation in the services offered by the institution to its customers (this varies considerably across institutions). The more differentiation, the more flexibility is needed and the more likely an institution is to source IT internally or closer to the business.

When the decision is made to outsource, it can be done for cost and/or quality (risk) reasons. Depending on the capability of the institution and the service provider, the outsourced arrangement (in stable state) can be more or less risky than the original in-house environment.

There is risk itself in making a transition to a service provider. Two big drivers of risk are the change process itself and new exposures due to geographic and/or jurisdiction changes. The more elements of service provision that are changing, the more the risk increases. Are people changing? Are processes changing? Is equipment changing?

In both the transition and steady state, a key question that must be constantly asked is: **What is different?** This is especially important with cloud services. This starts with how the economic model is different. A third-party service provider exists because it can earn a profit on service provision. To earn that profit it must be more efficient and effective than its customers. This means acquiring resources (people, hardware, software) at lower costs and providing them more efficiently (largely through automation and improved processes). As a practical matter, the focus is on lower cost people through off-shoring and process quality.

In an outsourcing arrangement, a financial institution cannot transfer the risk of failures in operations to the third party-only operations. Depending on relative capability, this may reduce risk. Legally, to regulators, customers and partners, the risk is still faced. While the institution can seek financial recovery from the third party, the risks still exist.

Thus, for the operational risk leader working with the IT-related risk manager and the CIO, the question becomes how to properly evaluate and assure performance in third-party service providers.

Typical contracts are written around performance measures, often termed 'service levels'. They also should contain provisions for auditing and damages for failing to achieve service within the stated tolerance.

Contracts will likely also include provisions for performance against compliance requirements that existed at the time the contract was written.

From a risk management perspective, there are two weaknesses with this approach:

1. First, risk management looks for leading indicators. These are found by measuring capability (such as oversight quality, process quality, training or certifications of employees). Measuring capability is key because it is a leading indicator of problems. So capability should be considered along with outcomes—this is the same as in any service, from flying airplanes to building houses.

2. Second, compliance requirements have changed dramatically in recent years, leaving service providers reeling in the face of standard contract language that they must comply with the legal requirements faced by their customers. This puts financial strain on the service provider's low-cost financial model.

For the risk manager, this means the need to foster a tight linkage between the internal business customer and the service provider personnel actually touching the relevant systems, so as to create an ongoing dialogue around the level of risk and actions to manage it.

This is especially important in areas such as application development, where outsourcing (especially off-shoring) breaks typical best practices in agile application development when the users, administrators and developers are intentionally separated and compartmentalized to reduce cost. This is an advantage when the business goal is scalable cost savings. It is a disadvantage when the business goals are flexibility in financial product design and time-to-market.

It also means carefully selecting the right evaluation approach.

The good news is that there are several good guidance documents available to help evaluate service providers. ISACA's *Risk IT* can be used to evaluate a service provider's quality of risk management, just as it was used within the institution. To get to the core of the IT operations, more is needed. This is where COBIT directly comes into play as the 'Rosetta stone' of IT management guidance. COBIT is not only for managers, but (with supporting guidance) is already used by auditors and examiners. It includes specific guidance on third-party service providers (found in the Deliver and Support domain). This can be used to evaluate the maturity and quality of IT management activities to reduce risk.

Other guidance

Several other key guidance documents map to COBIT.

The BITS/Financial Services Roundtable Shared Assessment Program was originally designed as a cooperative assessment approach between financial institutions and service providers.

The program created two key documents. The Structured Information Gathering (SIG) tool is a long list of self-evaluation questions to be used by service providers (and optionally shared with customers). The Agreed Upon Procedures can be thought of as a limited-purpose audit that tests the existence (but not quality) of service provider polices and procedures.

They are available for free download at **www.sharedassessments.org**. The program is member-driven and the author team is always looking for new members and contributors. Make sure you use the current version as it is improved each year.

Those of us who have helped create this content have also provided mappings to COBIT, the *US FFIEC IT Examination Handbooks* and other content (for example, in security, to the ISO 27001:2005 Annex A Controls). In addition, the AUPs are designed to provide added strength to an evaluation based on the International Federation of Accountants International Auditing and Assurance Standards Board (IAASB) International Standards on Auditing (ISA) 3402. In the US, the AICPA has issued the Statements on Standards for Attestation Engagements (SSAE) 16 which is substantially similar to the 3402. Other countries also have national versions. The AICPA's additional guidance booklet is helpful. The predecessor American Institute of Certified Public Accountants (AICPA) Statements on Auditing Standards (SAS) 70 was designed to evaluate IT with a view to providing reasonable assurance that financial statements could be properly produced. The 3402/SSAE 16 added an option for a separate engagement to evaluate operations. As the IAASB 3402/SSAE 16 is new, time will tell how it is implemented. A COBIT-based evaluation, with its longer history of use and more robust supporting guidance, is a more 'known' choice for careful reviews.

To go deeper on how IT management processes should work, the best choice is the IT Infrastructure Library (ITIL), from the UK's Office of Government Commerce (OCG) and supported by the IT Service Management Forum (itSMF). This and the corresponding ISO/IEC standard (20000) provide guidance on management processes such as release, availability or configuration management. The COBIT to ITIL mapping can be found at **www.isaca.org/COBITmappings**.

To go deeper in specific areas, such as security, the COBIT mappings provide a significant resources base. While the perspective in these documents is that of an IT manager or practitioner, their guidance is also entirely applicable to an examiner, auditor or risk management leader; much can be gained simply by reading the guidance as a series of 'Do you do…?' questions that can be asked of a service provider.

* * *

In summary, the operational risk leader needs to know that IT-related business risk is substantial risk to the increasingly automated financial institution. The need is to remember that many institutions seek to save costs by outsourcing aspects of information systems to service providers, and that transitioning to a service provider (like most changes) brings risk. In steady state, these arrangements can have more or less risk than the current environment. The amount of risk is largely dependent on people and process quality. To evaluate a third-party's quality of risk management and IT operations management, a wealth of well-developed guidance is available. Operational risk leaders should focus on ensuring that IT-related business risk managers are using the appropriate guidance in an appropriate way to make risk management more efficient and effective, and to reduce risk to operations.

Key points

- Financial institutions are heavily dependent on IT.

- Operational risk leaders must ensure that IT-related business risk management crosses the many IT silos and is deeply integrated into broader operational risk.

- Constantly scrutinize change for how the process brings risk in both implementation and operations, and seek to shape IT change to reduce risk to the business.

2.7. React and Recover—Right Action at the Right Time

Risk to operations management cycle

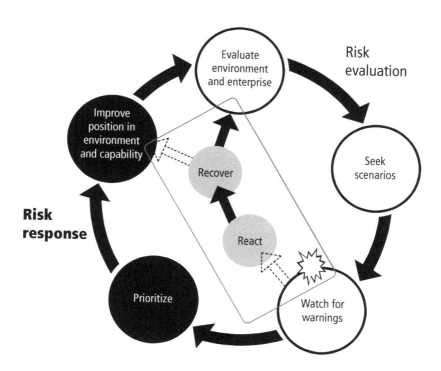

Figure 39

When a problem or event in the system threatens business performance, a reaction is required. The reaction loop of the risk management cycle is followed. In reacting, options are limited to *existing* capabilities (resources, plans, oversight, management, controls and processes to use them) such as extra servers, investigators or crisis teams. For example, an institution can degrade operations in the event of a cyber-attack, close branches in the event of bad weather, or deploy a pre-defined 'SWAT'-style team to address a system outage.

React to cascading events

In seminars, I ask participants to imagine being asked after an incident: 'Who knew?', 'When?' and 'What did they do?' Whether fraud, cyber-attack, systems outage, data loss or product problems, the questions are the same. There is a rich literature on incident responses from a wide range of disciplines (crisis management, medical response, cyber-threat response, industrial safety, supply chain management [logistics and selecting sourcing locations by risk], IT operations and more). Observing organizations around the world, three factors influence success in minimizing damage: time, preparation, and decision-making.

Time

Time concerns length of warning, when the problem occurred relative to other events, and duration. For example, how long was data being stolen before it was discovered? When in the day, week or month were the suspicious trades typically executed? For example, did the software application go down during quarterly close? **The key elements of time must be understood**, to not only create a life-like scenario but also to improve the ability to watch for warnings, design controls, prepare to react, and strengthen capabilities.

Preparation

How mature are the organization's capabilities? Were root-cause problems identified in risk evaluation actually fixed in a timely manner and tested during the prevention phases? Is the chain of command clear in reacting to a risk? Who has the authority to stop something bad from continuing? Do they know it? Will they act? How will the right information get to the right people at the right time? Who is accountable? When taking action, how does the decision-maker know what the correct action is? What amount of loss was pre-defined as acceptable to trigger action?

Failure to prepare to react has led to many high-profile failures, from errors in corporate investigations to industrial accidents.

Decision-making

Front-line information must integrate with executive ability to act to face the situation. Fascinating insight comes from reading post-incident reviews (PIRs) on the websites of organizations such as the North American Electric Reliability Corporation, US National Transportation Safety Board, the US Chemical Safety Board, or reports on financial institution solvency. Once the alarm goes off, command and control tools take center stage in the risk management process. This draws on a large body of knowledge from crisis management, disaster recovery and emergency response.

Command and control systems include several elements:

- roles for people and teams
- key information and communications channels
- processes for accomplishing objectives
- support and supply structures
- decision criteria/rules to simplify actions that need to be taken.

Examples of systems include:

- US National Incident Command System, including how organizations such as financial institutions work in crisis situations in coordination with many other types of responders to play their role in public response and resume their own internal operations. Online courses are available at **www.fema.gov**. The US Federal Emergency Management Agency (FEMA) Incident Command System (ISC) 100 course is online. It takes about three hours to complete and is recommended both for general knowledge and to help you and your institution interact with public safety officials during a disaster. The ICS is just one of three elements, along with Multiagency Coordination and Public Information of the US National Incident Management System (NIMS) Command and

Management component. The NIMS components of Preparedness, Communications and Information Management, and Resource Management provide a framework for effective management during incident response.[43]

- OCEG (Open Compliance and Ethics Group)'s Governance, Risk and Compliance Capability Model 2.0's section on 'Respond and Resolve' that includes guidance on investigations, crisis response and recovery. The *Redbook* is a free download at **www.oceg.org**.

A full treatment of command and control tools is beyond the scope of this book. Here, it's important to ask yourself two questions:

1. Do you have the 'been there, done that' capabilities (skills and processes) to build action plans—your plan B?

2. Have you made a difference in your organization because you led risk owners to **put plans in place to react more quickly and appropriately to a range of operational situations**? Just as a manager of market risk provides business value by taking immediate action to change a position, a manager of operational risk must be ready to take action when the alarm rings.

Three examples help illustrate this:

The headline screamed: "There Was 'Nobody in Charge'—After the Blast, Horizon Was Hobbled by a Complex Chain of Command; A 23-Year-Old Steps In to Radio a Mayday." The *Wall Street Journal* account of the first few minutes of the BP Deepwater Horizon disaster is sobering; investigations are still underway and key information was lost with the people who died. **Risk management is about action—responding, not just evaluating. The right actions matter**.[44]

In the town of Otsuchi in Iwate Prefecture, Japan, it was widely reported that Mayor Koki Kato died after being washed away by the tsunami during an outdoor emergency meeting held shortly after the March 11 2011 quake.

In a financial context, the business press has documented chains of events where making risk-aware decisions has helped and hurt. For example,

---

[43] More information on NIMS can be found at **www.fema.gov/emergency/nims**.

[44] *Wall Street Journal* (May 27 2010), **on.wsj.com/92pKY6**.

Businessweek ran a mini-series in their June 22 2009 issue entitled "The Risk Takers," discussing decisions at several enterprises.[45] In another example, *Businessweek*'s April 1 2010 story on Goldman Sachs reports on key decisions made by the firm to avoid potential loss, such as when Goldman went neutral on mortgages. These and other stories highlight decisions to react to an environment in view of enterprise capabilities and how planning helped them prepare for those decisions.

Recover from damage

The *react* step seeks to contain, slow or stop an unfolding cascade of events. Each step of the cascade had an impact and resulted in consequences that are financial, operational, customer-satisfaction-related, reputational, legal and more.

Once the cascade has significantly slowed or stopped, the *recover* step comes to efficiently and effectively rebuild. Actions include: rebuilding physical capability; compensation to harmed persons; internal correction and rework; liability settlements; regulatory fines; contractual penalties; and advertising and media relations.

The recovery step builds on actions taken earlier. It uses planning and organizational tools such as the incident-management team.

Rapid recovery in *process-related* situations largely depends on three factors:

1. finding the root cause quickly, based on understanding how the process works and having controls close to the source of the problem

2. the strength of the underlying process capability

3. being prepared with procedures and resources to make repairs.

Rapid recovery in *environment-related* situations largely depends on three factors:

1. the command and control capabilities described in the react section

2. clear procedures that can be implemented by primary or back-up people

3. replacement/additional resources.

---

[45] **buswk.co/16ISea.**

This applies whether the environmental change is a natural disaster, a case of social unrest, cyber-attack, accidental damage, a surprise political announcement or unexpectedly high trading volume that is stressing capacity. Longer-term environment changes (legal, economic, technological, demographic) were addressed earlier in the chapter on improvements.

Specific recovery actions depend on the nature of the environment or process change that occurred, how it unfolded, how quickly it unfolded, and what assets/resources were impacted in the financial institution. For environment changes, systemic impacts to suppliers, partners, competitors and customers would also change the nature of the recovery actions.

Rebuilding can be a stand-alone endeavor if the resources are specific to the damage done (clean a flooded building, pay damages to customers, pay fines). However, when rebuilding is more extensive, then it is often more cost-effective to combine the rebuilding with larger capability improvement projects. For example, one institution had repeated problems in wealth management. Rather than address these as individual regulatory responses, it was more cost-effective to clean up the process end-to-end with improved product-management discipline.

Due to this range of potential actions for recovery, the needed subject matter expertise will also vary—a cyber-security, media relations, disaster recovery, or country general manager might be leading the recovery.

The role of the operational risk leader is to support the leader on point in the immediate recovery and then foster improvement in the react and recovery steps in the future. Thus, the **tools that are most helpful to the operational risk management leader are those that look across the entire unfolded situation** to all impacted areas to ask and answer the questions—What went wrong? How did we do? What was missed that needs to be addressed immediately? And how can we improve in future? Two tools are helpful.

Post-incident reviews (PIRs)

These analyses start at root cause, track unfolding events, document actions taken and measure loss (including opportunity loss). In understanding actions taken, it looks at what was done when. PIRs can be made easier by drawing on the dependency analysis and root-cause analysis conducted during risk evaluation. Examples of PIRs can be found on a variety of industry organization and government websites. These include the North American

Electric Reliability Corporation (**www.nerc.com**), the US Chemical Safety Board (**www.csb.gov**), and the US National Transportation Safety Board (**www.ntsb.gov**). Others include analyses prepared by your legal counsel for litigation or regulatory actions, and case studies from professional associations.

Business action change analysis

This looks at the implications following an incident or (indeed especially) a series of incidents.

It is primarily intended for the board of directors, board risk committee and senior management.

The analysis looks across all the incidents and post-incident reviews over a period of time and asks: 'What are we doing differently?' Have negative incident patterns been corrected?

If patterns of bad outcomes are persisting, improvements are discussed at the level of a) core business product process, b) controls, c) management process and d) oversight—based on root-cause analysis and PIRs.

This approach is especially helpful to understand if the board's own action/inaction, risk oversight or risk culture are hurting efforts to achieve an improved risk–return balance. (More on this can be found in part 3 on risk oversight.)

The operational risk leader difference

Manage options

Document lessons learned, assign values to options that would have helped react or contain the unfolding problem more quickly.

Find balance

Help the organization define how quickly it will react in the presence of a warning. In routine situations (such as market price changes) organizations are more comfortable reacting. In unusual situations, organizations can delay, waiting for more information while the problem grows (as was the case for many investors in August to October of 2008).

Create levers

First, create guidance to link warnings to action. As in trading, rules (shaped by scenario analysis) remove hesitation and indecision. Second, apply lessons broadly enough to prevent similar problems. When lessons are applied narrowly, the institution is surprised by similar problems, as in rogue trader losses.

Design solutions

Invite the right people to PIRs to define and build buy-in for improvement.

Key points

- Risk management is not just about evaluation; it's about acting on the risks.

- Use tools to look across the entire chain of unfolded events to avoid similar future problems.

- The pain suffered creates value when it prevents future problems and makes better decisions.

2.8. Key Insights for Responding to Risk

In the risk management process cycle, scenarios and warnings were the inputs to responding to risk. In responding, the normal loop repositions/reshapes within the environment and builds capabilities. In doing so, risk managers bring something special to the cross-discipline party to improve business outcomes. Risk-prioritization tools enhance business performance, process and quality improvement approaches. The reaction loop draws on emergency and investigative approaches to contain, slow and stop a cascade of events. Then recovery begins. After building from the normal loop or rebuilding from the reaction loop, the cycle comes back to the foundation of evaluating the environment and enterprise. Together, the cycle finds and fixes problems—delivering value.

Improvements in environment positioning and enterprise capability support the aspirations of *A Revised Framework*. Improvements can be reflected in the core capital requirement and (for risk governance and management process improvements) in the Pillar 2 adjustment. This does not mean the total capital requirement will be lower if other factors are acting to increase capital. The point is to **have a direct linkage for reflecting actual risk reduction in capital requirements**.

In summary, key insights from the chapters on responding to risk are:

- As the institution's risk management matures, emphasis shifts from finding risks to fixing them.

- In responding to risk, understand your options and the value of keeping them open to respond to risk. Scrutinize decisions that would foreclose your options to prevent or react to risk.

- Time matters—understand the implications at each step of the cycle.

- Take advantage of the wide range of proven approaches to reduce risk from disciplines such as business process improvement/reengineering, quality control, software application development, business continuity, crisis management, strategic planning and financial management.

- Select from the range of tools/techniques to help clarify risk-response priorities for action.

- Tools are ways to make capability improvement easier. Capability improvements are levers (in both the risk management and competitive strategy sense) for outcomes improvements. Create levers!

- Make the distinction between responses to risks that are environment-related (usually external and non-process driven), and those that are process-related.

- Make a distinction between strengthening capabilities in oversight, management, controls and the business-product process (*analyze, develop, market, sell, deliver, support*).

- Partner with other teams in the institution with objectives to improve process, grow profitable revenue and/or protect from risk.

- Efficient and effective 'command and control' capabilities are crucial to being able to react fast enough to minimize loss or take advantage of opportunity.

- Once a problem occurs, the focus is on slowing or stopping the cascade of events to reduce the impact and consequences. Success in this reduction is dependent on underlying business process capability, preparedness, controls and early warning situational awareness.

- Rapid recovery largely depends on quickly finding the root cause of a change, understanding environment and/or process, and advance preparations for recovery.

- Improvements over the longer term are the only true way to achieve risk reduction. Heroic, shorter-term fixes are needed to stay in business, but efficient risk response depends on improvements in capabilities and positioning within or reshaping the environment.

- Understanding controls in basic terms makes it easier to make controls more effective in finding and fixing problems and more efficient to implement, maintain and test.

- Product-management discipline can help engage the institution to reduce a range of risks, such as fraud, while improving business outcomes.

- IT risk grows as institutions become more dependent on technology. Established tools can help you map dependencies, and avoid product and process problems.

- Your opportunity as an operational-risk leader is to harness a range of proven tools, and engage well-trained people to: 1) use risk management insight to apply this capability to the top priorities for risk reduction and 2) lead the team to solutions that are faster, better and cheaper than would have occurred otherwise. This creates shareholder value.

We've now completed our tour of the risk management process cycle. We've encountered many ways to improve the efficiency and effectiveness of operational risk management to improve business performance, and compliance. In the next two chapters, we step back to look at the role of risk oversight in guiding, improving and monitoring both risk management and its own self-improvement.

Part 3.
Oversight of Risk Management

3.1. Oversight of Risk Management

"Problems start when decision-makers' perspectives are too narrow—they don't have all the necessary information and, worse, don't realize they need to broaden their view. Managers believe they are making correct decisions from their own, limited, perspective. But they may not be correct in a higher operational context. I encourage risk managers to look for the conditions of poor decisions. People on the front lines are more likely to have the details, but less likely to understand corporate objectives. The boardroom knows the objectives, but must work to get full clarity on operations and the implications of that status. Risk managers can help bring this together."

— *Rick Sergel*

Business objective

The *business objective* of risk oversight is to improve risk-adjusted return by *making more risk-aware business decisions* supported by risk management practices that are used daily in the enterprise. The *tests of quality* are whether a) the board and all levels of management are making decisions that appropriately balance risk and return and b) the risk oversight and management processes are being continually improved.

On the quest for meeting this objective, institutions encounter many hurdles:

- lack of clarity on what such success looks like—better business results from more risk-aware decisions

- finding the 'pain' (problems) in the risk management process

- insufficient knowledge or action from the board

- confusion between 'governance' and 'management'

- surprises by external audit and regulatory findings

- uncertainty in completing public company risk disclosures

- uncertainty in evaluating board risk capability or the operational risk management function

- difficulty in achieving a 'fix that sticks' for repeat problems.

Make more risk–return-aware business decisions

Achieving better outcomes more efficiently and effectively is easier, again, with a focus on key points:

- Governance is about getting the right information to the right people at the right time to make the right (or at least better) decisions.

- We say 'better' rather than 'right' decisions, because there is a cost/benefit of information.

- Governance, strictly speaking, is about board-of-directors' oversight of management. Governance can also be formally delegated to bodies of managers, especially for oversight of initiatives or resources that cross silos within the institution.

- The oversight (governance) cycle, with its layers of corporate, business, risk and operational-risk governance, is distinct from the risk management cycle and the institution's core-business product-process cycle. Problems in each of these cycles must be understood and fixed to have healthy risk management that drives performance and achieves compliance with laws, regulations and contracts.

- More risk–return-aware decisions that better balance risk and return is the key process objective. This is supported by a common view of risk, standard risk analysis templates and risk budgets.

- Risk culture is crucial: It can tear down or support risk management success. Culture is measured in specifics. One key measure is the attitude toward finding and fixing fast. Culture that discourages finding and reporting problems quickly (regardless of formal policy) is a danger.

- Operational risk management is embedded into enterprise-wide risk management and business management by connecting the dots with related organizational bodies, processes and communication flows. Risk management is embedded into operations when front-line managers daily make more risk–return-aware decisions. Finding and fixing problems on the front-lines is usually more efficient and effective than layering on more controls and audits.

- Risk governance and risk management are evaluated with specific tools. An example is the governance health check that evaluates whether governance is informed, transparent, accountable and agile. All evaluations must focus on finding and fixing true root causes.

Begin with basics to get to the benefit

The benefits of better risk oversight are demonstrated in better business returns, because the institution has been superior at *positioning itself in a risky world* and *allocating resources to capabilities* that enable it to grow profitable revenue—all the while complying with requirements. Many institutions struggle to achieve these benefits because they struggle with how to make more risk–return-aware decisions. Decision processes are a key element of governance. Because institutions can churn for days, weeks or months on what 'governance' is, it might be helpful for some to make this clear.

It's not so much that governance is muddy as it is that governance has multiple (and often precise) meanings.

Selected perspectives and definitions on governance include:

- legal: what governors must do, may do and should not do

- organization design: organizational bodies (also called 'structures'), processes and communication

- decision science: decision rights and roles relating to: responsibility, accountability, consultation, information

- policy: culture, values, mission, structure and layers of policies, processes and measures

- audit: control.

To start simple, consider a little shop. The woman who owns the shop directly manages her few employees. As her business grows, she hires people and is open longer hours. She hires her first manager. She is now in the role of owner, governing the manager to ensure the manager does what she would have done. The tendency of the manager (agent) to act in self-interest, rather than the owner's (principal) interest, is 'the principal-agent problem'. This also arises in rogue trading, where a trader, not seeking to be malicious, takes on risk in excess of the limits of the board of directors and shareholders.

Board members represent owners. They provide oversight of management and make key business decisions (strategy, M&A, process, personnel).

One of the more frequently quoted definitions of corporate governance is from the Organization for Economic Co-operation and Development (OECD).

The mission of the OECD is to promote policies that will improve the economic and social well-being of people around the world. The OECD corporate governance principles (2004) state:

> "Corporate governance involves a set of relationships between a company's management, its board, its shareholders and other stakeholders.

> "Corporate governance also provides the structure through which the objectives of the company are set, and the means of attaining those objectives and monitoring performance are determined [sic]. Good corporate governance should provide proper incentives for the board and management to pursue objectives that are in the interests of the company and its shareholders and should facilitate effective monitoring.

> "Corporate governance is one key element in improving economic efficiency and growth as well as enhancing investor confidence."[46]

In this definition, notice the emphasis on performance and investors. It is not just about compliance and controls.

Governance also takes on a stretched meaning when it is used in a delegated sense. To corporate attorneys, the only real governance comes from the shareholders, board of directors and chair of the board. The CEO, president and all other executives are *management*. Yet, in common usage 'governance'

---

[46] bit.ly/pUf0F.

is applied to a range of cross-silo coordination activities in the enterprise, including intellectual property, risk, IT, business continuity and a number of temporary projects. To be legitimate, such governance must operate under a delegated charter from, and be accountable to, a higher body—ultimately the board.

* * *

To bring clarity in word usage and focus on outcomes, this simple definition of governance is therefore suggested: '*Getting the right information to the right people at the right time to make the right decisions with accountability.*'

In practice, 'right' decisions become 'better' decisions, in order to reach a balance between the cost of studying a decision and the likely improvement in decision quality it could bring.

Supporting this definition are the three elements of governance: bodies, process and communication (or, more broadly, 'leadership').

Elements of governance

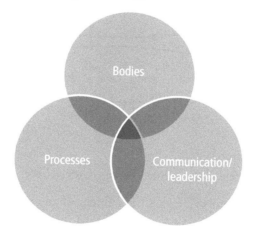

Governance should overcome limitations of organization structure to improve speed, coordination and efficiency.

Figure 40

Another area that can benefit from clarity is sorting out how governance is different from management.

Again, a key point is that governance when performed by managers is a) delegated down by the shareholders/board and b) performed in the interest of the enterprise as a *whole*, distinct from the person's role managing a business line, function or regional area.

When governance of functional areas (such as risk management) is discussed this can be further complicated. This is because risk (like finance, HR or sales) involves both its own process and touches others. To keep your whiteboards from becoming a jumble of action items, group them into three cycles of activities.

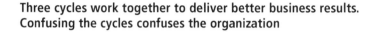

Three cycles work together to deliver better business results. Confusing the cycles confuses the organization

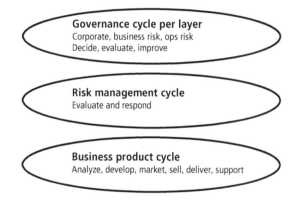

Figure 41

The governance cycle is the subject of this discussion.

The risk management cycle was the subject of the earlier discussions on evaluating risk and responding to risk. Here it is addressed in the context of oversight.

The business-product cycle (analyze, develop, market, sell, deliver, support) was addressed earlier in the context of leveraging product management to reduce risk to operations. This cycle is an important interlock, where functional (including shared services) and geographically aligned management come together to focus on business products.

In each of these cycles, oversight by a governance body (of board members or delegated to senior managers) may be used.

When the governance cycle is applied to operational risk management, four layers make it more specific to operational risk:

- **Corporate governance** is the board of directors both overseeing risk management and making its own risk-return balanced decisions..

- **Business governance** refers to a structure composed of senior managers, acting as a group *in the interest of the enterprise as a whole* (as opposed to their individual managerial roles). This is delegated by the board of directors.

- **Risk governance** provides oversight to all risk management activities, *in the interest of the enterprise as a whole*. This is delegated by the board of directors' risk oversight committee.

- **Operational risk governance** provides oversight to all operational risk management activities, in the interest of the enterprise as a whole. This is delegated by an enterprise-wide management risk oversight committee.

Notice that each layer has a specific purpose, delegation of authority and members. It will also have processes and communication—both within its body and connecting to other bodies. **A key benefit of healthy governance is that it helps cross silos to make better decisions, in the interest of the enterprise, faster**.

Board skills and safeguards

To achieve the benefits, it is becoming more popular, sometimes required, to create a risk committee of the board of directors to focus board members with sufficient skill on the institution's risk management. Depending on country and industry, regulators require disclosures to shareholders on risk management practices and risk skills of board members. Keys to success are sufficient skill and focus.

Diverse skill

We've seen the struggles of enterprises that lack a systematic approach to and skills in risk. This also applies to boards. For example, the skill an audit committee member might have in risk-based audits is only one view on risk. For boards to exercise oversight and make their own risk-return balanced decisions, it is helpful to grow in two ways.. First, diverse experience in both industries and risk disciplines—supply-chain risk management, hospital risk management, military or civil preparedness, technology-risk management, strategic or new-products risk can all make valuable contributions to the risk committee. Second, **training in open, recognized best practices for risk management**. **Board members cannot ask penetrating questions to probe for gaps without a solid** benchmark of what is 'good'.

Proactive focus

The members of the risk committee (like any other committee) must have time to be *proactive* in their assignment. Extra time is needed because the risk management committee is likely to be newer and be operating in a changing business and legal environment. **The risk committee members must have time to proactively address each of the three cycles where risk management is concerned** (governance, risk management and business product) to ask probing questions and ensure that daily risk–return-aware decisions are being made that are aligned with shareholder interests and compliance requirements. This includes critiquing the risk-return balanced decision-making of the board and catalyzing education as needed.

Risk management audit independence

As boards form risk committees and organizations strengthen risk management, a question is more frequently raised about the interaction of the risk management and audit functions at both the board and management levels. As one regulator said: "Independent review—that's a key item we bring up." Drawing on several sets of industry guidance, these are key points:

At the managerial level:

- The audit function must remain independent of management. They cannot create or manage some aspect of risk management and then conduct an independent audit.

- Risk management can be helped by audit to reduce fragmentation.

- Internal audit 'findings' are an input to the risk-assessment process. Risk management must remain independent of business-line, functional or geographic management. They cannot own the actual risk. Like finance, risk management is a support function; it assists operating units in achieving objectives in an area of specialty.

- Risk management must remain independent of audit. They cannot risk-assess audit if they designed audit's risk assessments, report to audit or audit reports to risk management.

- This said, especially in smaller institutions, there is simply a lack of skill to go around. In these cases, audit or risk management departments may assist business-line management in limited capacities. The individuals who provide that assistance should not take ownership of risk or provide the evaluations. Such situations should also be communicated to the board for approval.

- Internal audit should leverage the risk identification, evaluation, monitoring, and remediation program.

- Audit can be helped by risk management to improve the scope of audits.

At the board level:

- The independent voices of both chief risk officers and chief audit executives need to be heard by the board. They are both safeguards of shareholder interests. The skill of the individuals and their vantage points will hopefully cause them to have unique insights. Board members should seek to bring this out and set the expectation that 'the board wants to know'.

- The board should recognize the different missions of audit and risk management functions. The risk officer is seeking to ensure that the risk–return balance is achieved in business decisions in accordance with the board's direction. The chief audit executive is primarily seeking to provide assurance of compliance with controls (defined by internal policy, regulation or law). Failures in controls will likely increase risk. Good risk management will incorporate good controls. Yet risk management will also involve questions about the judgment of business decisions and actions that are often outside the scope of typical audits, because risk management is a managerial function intended to be used daily for business decisions.

- Have separate risk and audit committees.[47] Internationally, the Basel Committee strongly guides towards separate committees. For banks with more than $10 billion in assets covered by the US Dodd-Frank law, a

---

[47] Bank for International Settlements. (October 2010), 'Principles for enhancing corporate governance'.

separate risk committee with at least one member who is a risk expert is required. The Federal Reserve Board is authorized to extend this to non-banks and smaller banks. Practically, separate committees give more ears on the board to hear the independent voices of the risk and audit managers and enable the creation of a risk committee comprised of members with knowledge of a diverse range of risks—operational, strategic, market, product, country and such. This avoids a narrow view of risk, such as risk primarily to financial statements or controls that often occupies the audit committee.

- Boards with the discretion to use a combined audit and risk committee would be wise to pay special attention to two points. First, regulators are often quick to note that reliance on key board members to oversee both audit and risk creates a 'key person'-dependency risk. Second, the importance of all other independence safeguards significantly increases.

- Additional guidance on the relationship between risk management is available from several sources. From a regulatory perspective, the primary reference is in Section 666 of Basel II A Revised Framework. General guidance is available from the Institute of Internal Auditors.[48] The UK Financial Services Authority and Bank of England have a code of practice for auditors and bank supervisors.

Key points

- Risk management only matters if it is *used daily to make better decisions*.

- Simplify the many types of actions by grouping them into cycles of activities—risk governance/oversight, risk management and business-product processes.

- Risk management and audit functions must be independent of each other and of business-line owners of risk.

---

[48] The Institute of Internal Auditors. (2004), 'The Role of Internal Auditing in Enterprise-wide Risk Management'. (London & Altamonte Springs).

3.2. Four Functions of a Governor

"Understanding and responding to risk all comes together in the board. Institutions of all sizes must provide oversight that integrates in several ways. They must ensure that risks are being interrelated—market, credit, operational and liquidity—both inside and outside of the institution. Looking outside is crucial to avoid catching a systemic risk contagion. They must ensure that risk management is being used in daily decisions by all managers. Next, they must consider whether their own skills and governance are sufficient for the task—and report on this as part of new regulations. Finally, they must set the example by pushing on risks in each decision that comes to the board."

— *Mark Olson*

Different professional bodies of knowledge (e.g. legal, organizational or performance) and other guidance documents, assign somewhat different responsibilities to a governor. The Bank for International Settlements (BIS) guidance, 'Principles for enhancing corporate governance', is based on the OECD guidance mentioned in chapter 3.1. Yet, a board member should not view this as a compliance check box. Indeed, BIS states: "The board and senior management are primarily responsible and accountable for the governance and *performance* of the bank, and shareholders should hold them accountable for this." (paragraph 132; emphasis added). Stepping back entirely from regulation, a board is expected to create value through focus on strategy, people and decision-making process.

Thus, we focus here on four essentials to financial services operational risk management from an oversight perspective: decision-making; culture;

integration into enterprise-wide risk management; and evaluation of management's implementation of operational risk management.

Using risk management—daily decisions

Governors must set the example by making decisions that balance risk and return. Governors can also review management's use of risk-return aware decision-making and can incentivize balanced decisions through compensation.[49]

All participants in the decision process should have a clear expectation that (depending on role) they are providing information, making risk–return-aware decisions and/or managing to outcomes in light of risks. For this to work at the board level, information must flow easily. To avoid ambiguity that could lead to delay, it is valuable to pre-define a smooth and timely process. The corporate secretary can play a key role in achieving these outcomes.

Each level of decision-maker should look up to the higher levels and see a) decisions made in view of solid risk analyses and b) higher levels reviewing lower-level decisions for risk–return balance. Governors at all levels can make such decisions more easily with help from three tools: a common view of risk, standard risk-analysis templates, and risk budgets that accompany revenue and expense budgets for initiatives.

Making more risk-aware daily decisions is not only smarter business, it also provides evidence to satisfy the 'use test' created by regulators in countries such as the UK to evaluate how well risk management is actually used in an institution.

Common view of risk

A common view of risk includes common terminology, a common way of breaking down and describing risks (taxonomy), and common data storage. Details were discussed earlier in the chapter on risk management registers/databases. Other guidance is found in ISACA's *Risk IT* section on risk registers and in COSO's *Enterprise Risk Management—Integrated Framework* section on loss event databases. From a governance perspective,

---

[49] Bank for International Settlements (October 2010), 'Principles for enhancing corporate governance', speaks of compensation being symmetric with risk outcomes (especially principles 9 [in particular Section D] and 11).

the common view of risk provides a shared way to: a) communicate, b) aggregate risk across the enterprise, and c) determine when 'too much' risk is being taken or when more risk—with careful management—can be taken in pursuit of return. Oversight must manage this balance as it directly impacts an institution's share value.

Standard risk analysis templates

Templates bring value in two ways. First, they help by structuring decisions to avoid missing problems, opportunities or cost-effective risk responses. This information comes from the evaluations and responses created earlier. Second, they establish tangible expectations for all levels of the organization to make fact-based risk–return-aware decisions. To enforce these expectations, decision-makers must not accept risk analysis in decision packages that are token (or almost identical) from decision to decision. For example, a back-up page in a decision-making template that routinely states, 'customer take rate might be lower than expected…costs could overrun… time could overrun…laws may change' is not acceptable. Pre-defined decision processes (written down in templates) provide clarity to improve the speed and quality of decision-making.

Risk budget

As discussed in the chapter on prioritizing improvement, this is a relatively simple way to enhance revenue and expense budgets to highlight the risk considerations in accepting or rejecting a project. It can be conducted in several levels of depth, from color-coding categories to probability models with risk-adjusted cash flows.

Governors should set the expectation that the quality of tool use should continually improve.

Improve the culture

Culture has been touched on several times. The emphasis here is that **specific actions are needed to improve culture**. Culture is not an amorphous blob that magically improves on its own. Business culture (a person in a system) generally responds best to what is valued—by incentive or inspection. An example of a specific action is to build risk–return awareness into daily decisions. Another example is being proactive to remove biases and hesitations to act. Both approaches encourage people to ask 'what?' 'why?' and 'how?' and thus tangibly improve culture.

From a governance perspective, two important tasks are, first, to be accountable for the quality of risk culture, and, second, proactively evaluate it—starting at the front-line. Former BP CEO Tony Hayward's promise "when he took the job in 2007 to focus 'like a laser' on safety came back to haunt him after the explosion on the Deepwater Horizon rig killed 11 workers and unleashed a deep-sea gusher of oil".[50] BP stated that they had a formal policy where anyone could stop operations if needed. The question is whether people really felt they could do so without repercussion. Poor culture can kill good process.

Like anything, better evaluation comes with clarity. For evaluating culture, **a simple four-point evaluation asks people: What is your willingness to be alert to risk, communicate risk, plan for risk, and respond**?

Evaluations can look at cultural influences on specific steps in the risk evaluation and response process, including reducing bias, the realism of scenarios, or challenging distribution assumptions in capital estimation models. This considers the likelihood that people will ignore or assume away risks, or avoid opportunities for improvement.

Two insightful and quick measures of culture are to ask about 1) the excuses given for ignorance of risk, and 2) the attitude toward finding risks—spotting gaps in early warning systems or dangers in control data. **If people are culturally accustomed to risk ignorance or scared to report findings, that's a troubling sign**. The culture should encourage findings to be reported quickly under a policy of find early, fix fast. In one organization I came across a manager who was conducting unofficial reviews so that he could find problems without reporting them. It was a sad, but commendable, effort to do the right thing in the face of negative culture. As was mentioned in the lessons learned from hospitals, there should be no punishment for raising an item early (assuming the person did not act in a criminal manner). In financial services, policy-makers are particularly sensitive to this, as reflected in recent laws.

---

[50] Associated Press. (July 27 2010), 'BP replaces CEO Hayward, makes record loss'.

Timing matters. In any setting, delays can be disastrous. The board must ensure that scheduled and situation-driven reports are timely enough to be able to prevent problems or at least slow, contain or stop unfolding cascades of events. Board members must be conscious of their personal role in improving timing. In one bank, risk reports to the board had to be reduced to only 75 words, given in a certain format and passed through multiple management approvals. This dramatically weakened the board's ability to take timely action in the interest of shareholders. The board must set the right cultural expectations.

Guidance on culture and risk management tailored to managing IT-related risk to operations is available in the Culture section in ISACA's *Risk IT Framework* (**www.isaca.org/riskit**). Additional guidance on culture in a general governance and risk context is in the 'Context and Culture' section of OCEG's *Redbook 2.0* (**www.oceg.org**).

Integrate with enterprise risk management

In inviting me to present, the director of one institution said: "We really need to get an integrated view of risk, especially operational risk, as it seems to touch everything."

Governors must oversee and enable the integration of operational risk with enterprise-wide risk management. Integration is also an enabler of more risk-return-aware decisions, because of the interdependences among risk areas.

Managers of risk to operations must integrate in several directions:

- *Downward* with the various operational silos: fraud, business continuity, technology operations, recovery, facilities, physical and technology security.
- *Sideways* with other risk management functions: credit, market, strategic, and (for insurers) claims and underwriting.
- *Sideways* with other support functions with similar objectives to reduce risk: project management, business-process improvement, quality control.
- *Upwards*: enterprise-wide risk management, business management (line, functional areas and geography), and the board of directors.

Remember, governance is more than an organizational structure. Besides communication, it also includes processes connecting up, down and sideways. With these clarifications, improving operational risk management governance and connecting it to the rest of the institution is about connecting the dots.

ORM governance linkages

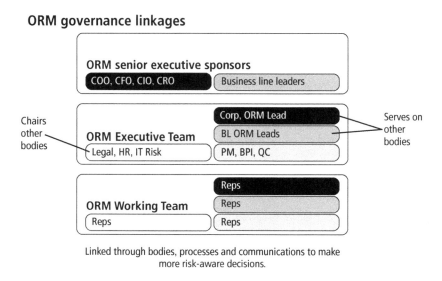

Linked through bodies, processes and communications to make more risk-aware decisions.

Figure 42

This example includes three organizational structures with distinct responsibilities, but a single goal:

- **ORM senior executive sponsors**—selected enterprise officers such as COO, CFO, CIO, and CRO, as well as selected business-line leaders, who would hold key roles on business and functional governance committees to embed risk awareness.

- **ORM executive team**—heads of operational risk at enterprise and business-line levels, plus key leaders of related areas including IT risk, business-process improvement, project management, HR, and legal.

- **ORM working team**—direct reports to the ORM executive team driving front-line execution.

Continuing the connect-the-dots analogy, the head of ORM would also join other governance committees for operations areas such as IT, human resources, business continuity, or new products. This dot-connecting should take place at both the enterprise and business-line levels.

Both the processes for governing *and* the processes being governed must account for risk so that ORM is efficient and effective. Doing so ensures that decisions are more risk–return aware.

To help operational risk management leaders achieve this integration more easily, the members of the enterprise-wide risk-oversight body, the business-oversight body and the board risk committee must all render aid and assistance. The body that created and delegated authority to the operational-risk oversight body—typically the enterprise-wide risk oversight body—needs to be on point to enable success. They are also responsible for enabling the interlock with the business-oversight body (often a senior management operating committee) to foster decisions to better balance risk and return. Ultimate oversight is by the board of directors.

From a best practices perspective, the closest guidance for integrating with enterprise-wide risk management is from ISACA's *Risk IT*. In that case, the guidance integrates IT-related business risk (including its operational aspects) into enterprise-wide risk management. It addresses five areas: Establish and maintain accountability for IT risk management; Coordinate IT risk strategy and business risk strategy; Adapt IT risk practices to enterprise risk practices; Provide adequate resources for IT risk management; and Provide independent assurance over IT risk management. This can be initially adapted to your needs in your institution, starting by replacing references to 'IT-related' with 'operational' risk and then adding the linkages mentioned above.

Three tips for integrating for more efficiency and effectiveness:

1. *Seek skills:* Teams in business-process improvement, enterprise architecture, quality control, product management and other areas are good at both finding and fixing problems. In fixing problems, their skills can design better solutions that gain more support from business leaders for not only reducing risk but also increasing business capability to sell and deliver products.

2. *Seek resources:* Team with other support functions to coordinate resources. More resources help achieve objectives more quickly.

3. *Clarify communications:* Create common terminology across the silos of operations-related risk management. As was noted earlier, each of these disciplines has years of history. Bridging terms together can make life easier for everyone.

Evaluate the quality of risk oversight. This is a make or break governance responsibility to self-assess and continually improve.

As a starting point, the four-element governance health check is a powerful and helpful tool.[51]

Transparent

- Is it easy to describe—do people know where to go and what to do?

- Does it provide the right information at the right time (visibility) to clarify tough decisions and prevent problems?

- Is it consistent in assigning roles and responsibilities to achieve desired outcomes?

Agile

- Does it operate with clear principles to reduce churn and debate?

- Does it move more quickly than, and overcome limitations of, formal 'solid line' organizational structures?

- Are meetings timely for making decisions?

- Does it provide clear and prompt escalation?

Informed

- Is it risk-aware, explicitly balancing risk and return?

- Does it balance the cost/benefit of improved information?

- Do policies 'stick' or are exceptions frequent?

- Does it represent those units providing requirements and resources?

- Does it balance focus across each step of the risk management process cycle?

---

[51] Health check used by permission of ValueBridge Advisors, LLC.

- Does it balance enterprise and business unit objectives?
- Does it addresses the entire process lifecycle and balance needed action in each stage of the lifecycle?

Accountable

- Does it assign clear accountability for each key decision type?
- Is it trusted to both help people make the right decisions *and* execute them well?
- Do performance measures cover key objectives—performance (financial, operational, customer-satisfaction), compliance, and capability building?

This can be tailored to your organization's design, circulated periodically to stakeholders, and the results reviewed in the oversight bodies. It is also helpful to do this *within* the board of directors to gain an appreciation of the extent to which other board members understand the risk discussions and are able to act on the information they hear.

As with other areas of the business, board member education is usually needed.

Beyond education, the boards may identify the need to add members with more diverse and deeper skills in risk management (now required in some jurisdictions). This includes experience in managing risk in operations outside financial services that can bring highly applicable new knowledge to the boardroom.

Tip: A frequent 'light bulb' moment with this health check is that **governance should improve agility**. Unless the institution needs to be less reckless, good governance should cross silos, bringing together people and information to make better decisions faster.

Caution: This health check is designed to evaluate the quality of the governance process itself, narrowly defined. While crucial and revealing, it is not all-sufficient. The board risk committee must also evaluate the risk management cycle to determine if the risk management function is helping business leaders daily make better decisions to better achieve shareholder objectives.

Evaluate management's implementation of risk management

The ultimate *outcome* objective of risk management is reducing risk to return. The ultimate *process* objective is making more risk-aware decisions to better balance risk and return in accordance with performance and compliance objectives.

To evaluate those ultimate objectives (especially in a way that helps pinpoint opportunities for improvement), a few key questions make a good start.

Were the desired outcomes achieved in:

- business lines (financial, operational, market position, customer satisfaction)?
- risk management (risks found, risks fixed, efficiency and effectiveness)?

Did each key cycle produce the desired outcomes in:

- risk oversight (governance)?
- risk management?
- business product processes?

Did the *enablers* mature in capability (skill, process and tools) as desired in:

- risk management?
- other risk-related supporting functions (e.g. business-process improvement, quality control, project management, architecture, business continuity, IT)?
- in the core product processes (product management, branch operations, clearing, brokerage and others)?

If not, why not?

The root-cause techniques discussed earlier in evaluating risk can be used here to diagnose the state of your institution's risk management process. For example, the 'five whys' provide a simple way to gain more precision more quickly. The reporting approaches suggested (such as reporting business outcomes, risk management outcomes and enabler status on the same page) make demonstrating improvement clearer.

Another simple tool is the accountability vs. avoidance health check. To use this, just ask:

One owner

Is there a single accountable owner for each task?

Explicit

Does the process make risks (especially new ones) explicit, timely and clear in decision-making?

Insight

Does it aggregate risks in a way that does not hide root causes and potential for occurrence in a mass of data?

Consistent

Is a similar measuring stick applied across multiple risks so they can be easily compared and prioritized?

Counted

Do analyses measure and include risks in a way that is meaningful by accounting for:

- all costs, including loss of potential?
- likelihood of risks?
- ability to detect risks (and not be blind-sided)?
- bias in estimation?

Understanding root causes is, of course, critical to fixing problems. From an oversight perspective, this means understanding where repeat weaknesses are due to problems in each of the three cycles. If oversight is the problem (including lack of knowledge and skill in the boardroom), then it is difficult for risk management and business-product cycles to compensate for that weakness.

Enhancing external reporting

Drawing together all the insights from risk evaluation, risk response, and the quality of risk management and oversight capability provides an opportunity to improve reporting for shareholders and regulators. This can be used to meet the needs of reporting required by the US SEC, UK Corporate Governance Code, and International Financial Reporting Standard 7.[52]

For shareholders, this information can **illustrate that the board 'gets it'— has the skill and focus, understands weaknesses, has identified opportunities for improvement and is taking action**. In an uncertain economic environment, this is especially important to communicate to investors. The ability to manage risks to operations in a changing environment has long been a differentiator. **Mandated disclosures provide an opportunity for institutions to showcase their capability. Performance is the proof**.

For regulators, it means comfort that the institution won't become a drain on deposit insurance funds or a cancer of systemic risk.

Key points

- Governors must set the example by making decisions that balance risk and return.

- Health checks evaluate governance. Governance should improve agility.

- Shareholder disclosures provide an opportunity to showcase high-quality risk management.

---

[52] The UK 'Walker Review' Recommendation 27 notes the linkage between strategy and risk.

3.3. Key Insights for Oversight and Governing Risk

Governance is about getting the right information to the right people at the right time to make the right (or at least better) decisions.

Governance, strictly speaking, is about board-of-directors' oversight of management. Governance can also be formally delegated to bodies of managers, especially for oversight of projects that cross silos within the institution.

The oversight (governance) cycle, with its layers of corporate, business, risk and operational-risk governance, is distinct from the risk management cycle and the institution's core business-product process cycle. Problems in each of these cycles must be understood and fixed to have healthy risk management that drives performance and achieves compliance with laws, regulations and contracts.

More risk–return aware decisions that better balance risk and return is the key process objective. This is supported by a common view of risk, standard risk analysis templates and risk budgets.

We say 'better', rather than 'right', decisions, because there is a balance of cost and benefit to be struck with such information.

Risk culture is crucial: It can tear down or support risk management success. Culture is **measured in specifics**. One key measure is the attitude toward finding and fixing problems quickly. Culture that discourages finding and reporting problems speedily (regardless of formal policy) is a danger.

Operational risk management is embedded into enterprise-wide risk management and business management by connecting the dots with related organizational bodies, processes and communication flows. **Risk management is embedded into operations when front-line managers daily make more risk–return-aware decisions**. Finding and fixing problems on the front-lines is usually more efficient and effective than layering on more controls and audit.

Risk governance and risk management are evaluated with specific tools. An example is the governance health check that evaluates whether governance is informed, transparent, accountable and agile. All evaluations must focus on finding and fixing true root causes.

Part 4.
You in Your Institution

4.1. Overcoming Barriers to Better Risk Management

What stands in the way of your getting more traction for your initiatives in your institution?

'It depends,' is the usual answer. To help you more easily diagnose your situation, these steps might help.

Evaluate the decision process

First, evaluate the decision process.

I once had a conversation with a risk management leader who wasn't getting sufficient support from her executive management. She had follow-up meetings where each time she tried to improve her description of a particular operational risk, she was frustrated that her management didn't 'get it'. Yet, in inquiring more closely, they actually did appreciate the problem, they just didn't support the solutions—or lack thereof. The solutions were not specific enough and had the potential to cost too much time and money.

Proposals for improvements to reduce risk sometimes need to be modified to accommodate changing conditions or business priorities, to share costs with some other initiatives (solving several problems with one fix) or to more fully capture benefits. Finally, sometimes it is a matter of whether the person(s) approving budget are really the ones with the problem. If a key executive who feels the pain is not part of the decision, sub-optimal decisions might be reached—for example, when regional business leaders are not included and decisions are made by 'headquarters', without consideration of local differences and issues created by pushing down a one-size-fits-all solution.

Evaluate capabilities

Second, evaluate capabilities.

Are there sufficient and necessary levels of awareness, process/methods, initial training, tools/techniques, ongoing training and automation in place? Building anything requires a plan, resources and capabilities. Where the capabilities are lacking, you will find failure.

Evaluate hurdles

Third, evaluate the hurdles faced at each stage of your initiative.

Some hurdles are about creating awareness of the problem. Organizations also are stymied at selecting the appropriate course of action. Still others can select a solution, but can never seem to launch the initiative. Others let initiatives wither and die; they don't have the follow-through to complete the project and reap the benefits. Understanding where resistance lies can help you more easily solve the problem.

Addressing these hurdles to success, you might wish to ask yourself these questions:

- Where does resistance exist in my organization?

- Why does it exist? (Is it inattention? Hopeful avoidance? Confusion in solution? People being haunted by past failure?)

- What is the problem? (It helps to state the problem in a formal way: *outcome* in *context* for *audience* due to *cause.*)

- How fast do we want to fix it?

- Which tools (from our discussion here) are most appropriate to use in addressing it? What else do we need?

- Who needs to be involved to achieve 'the fix'? (Think RACI.)

- What is the *next step* to traction?

- What resource is needed up-front to ensure *follow-through*?[53]

Armed with this information, you can start to create your personal action plan. Determine:

- top business risk–return value gaps

- change types causing the most risk

- risk categories most in need of improvement

- who feels the pain

- process and skill maturity gaps

- how much time you have to close gaps

- resources needed to close the gaps

- who owns the resources and whose approval is needed

- who needs to know the implications

- who will you engage and when to get needed expertise, including help to engage the executive team.[54]

In short, one key is to focus on business performance value (and compliance to the extent that it is assigned to operational risk management) to make a difference in areas like new revenue streams, M&A and efficiency drives. The second is to diagnose reasons for stalled progress and directly focus on moving those barriers, by harnessing the necessary resources and improving needed capabilities. Yes, this is easy to say and difficult to do. However, with the perspective, tools and guidance provided here, it will hopefully be much easier.

---

[53] Lists used by permission of ValueBridge Advisors, LLC.

[54] Lists used by permission of ValueBridge Advisors, LLC.

4.2. Your Questions for the Board of Directors

The board of directors both represents the shareholders and is legally responsible to regulators. They have the ability to provide clarity and focus as part of their oversight role. To do this effectively, boards must have breadth and depth of knowledge, as well as sufficient time to get further educated. Then they need to engage with management to provide the needed policy and direction.

To have a smoothly running operational-risk machine that is reducing risk to performance (and complying), the board members, business leaders, risk and operational-risk leaders must all have the education, knowledge, skills, tools and time to engage in the endeavor. Yet too often too many of these ingredients are missing. This leads to gaps, problems and then weaknesses in performance or compliance.

To help understand the perspective of those at the 'top of the business', we'll now have an exclusive question-and-answer session between some operational risk management leaders and financial institution board members, all of whom you will have met contributing their expertise earlier in the book.

Our panel is comprised of board members who certainly 'get' operational risk management. They are leaders who have fixed problems, enabled executives to be more successful and set higher standards throughout their careers.

So, in alphabetical order, let's meet our panel of expert board members.

Marshall N. Carter is chairman of NYSE Group, Inc. and deputy chairman of NYSE Euronext. From 1992–2001 Mr Carter was chairman and CEO of State Street Corporation. During his nine years as CEO, the company grew more than six fold to become a leading servicer and manager of financial pension and mutual fund assets worldwide. Prior to joining State Street, Mr Carter was with the Chase Manhattan Bank for 15 years, in positions related to finance, operations and global securities. Mr Carter is also past chairman of the board of trustees of the Boston Medical Center, and a lecturer at the Massachusetts Institute of Technology Sloan School of Management and Harvard's Kennedy School of Government. In 2006, Mr Carter was inducted into the American Academy of Arts and Sciences.

W. Ronald Dietz is chairman of the audit and risk committee of the board of directors of Capital One Financial. He has a broad background in general management and consulting. For the last nine years, until his recent retirement, he served as president and CEO of W.M. Putnam Company, an outsourcing company that assists nationally based companies and government entities in establishing, and maintaining, branch offices and retail stores across the US. Previously, Mr Dietz served as CEO of Anthem Financial and American Savings Bank of New York. He started his career at Citibank, where he moved through several senior assignments to become SVP and division executive in charge of Citibank's operations in the Caribbean and northern South America. Mr Dietz also serves as a senior advisor and board member to a variety of private companies and civic organizations. He earned an MBA from Stanford University.

Mark W. Olson served for five years as a member of the US Federal Reserve System Board of Governors and the Federal Open Market Committee. At the Federal Reserve Board, Mr Olson was the governor responsible for the internal risk management of the system. Later, he served as chairman of the Public Company Accounting Oversight Board; today he is co-chairman of Treliant Risk Advisors. Prior to his service at the Federal Reserve, he served as staff director of the securities subcommittee of the US senate committee on banking, housing and urban affairs. Mr Olson is also a past president of the American Bankers Association. Mr Olson has roots in community banking, beginning his career at First Bank System (now US Bancorp) and was ultimately named president and CEO of Security State Bank, a community institution founded by his father in 1957.

Karen R. Osar is a director of Webster Financial Corporation, a bank holding company of a $17+ billion bank, where she serves on the audit and risk committees. She is also a director of Innophos Holdings, a specialty chemicals manufacturer, SAPPI Ltd, a global pulp and paper company, and the Readers Digest Association. Ms Osar was the executive vice president and chief financial officer of Chemtura Corporation, a $4-billion specialty chemicals manufacturer, until her retirement in 2007. She previously served as senior vice president and CFO of MeadWestvaco Corporation, primarily a provider of packaging solutions and products. She also held the position of vice president and treasurer of Tenneco, Inc., a $12 billion industrial conglomerate. She began her career at JP Morgan where she rose to become managing director, investment banking. Ms Osar earned an MBA from Columbia.

Humphrey Polanen is a founding director of a *de novo* bank, Heritage Bank of Commerce. Headquartered in San Jose, California, Heritage was founded in 1994 and has grown to $1.3 billion in total assets. Mr Polanen came to the role with a background in technology, finance and law. He is presently chairman of uCirrus, a software company focused on the management of streaming data in enterprises and social networks, managing partner of Sand Hill Management Partners, chairman of St. Bernard Software and a leading international attorney. A former executive of Sun Microsystems for internet security, he is a graduate of Hamilton College and Harvard Law School.

Richard P. Sergel is a director of State Street Corporation and chair of the compensation committee. He served as president and chief executive officer of the North American Electric Reliability Corporation from 2005 until his retirement in 2009. Under legislative and regulatory authority from multiple governments in North America, NERC is the electric utility self-regulatory organization that sets and enforces mandatory reliability standards for the bulk power system in North America. Until 2004, Mr Sergel served as president and chief executive officer for National Grid USA, a large electric and gas utility. He was National Grid Group executive director for North America upon the completion of the National Grid and New England Electric System (NEES) merger in March 2000. From 1998 through the date of the merger, Mr Sergel was president and CEO.

Mr Sergel earned a BS in Mathematics from Florida State University, a Master of Science in Applied Mathematics from North Carolina State University, and an MBA from the University of Miami.

Do you see operational risk management as compliance assurance or as managing risks to performance?

If you do see operational risk management as primarily about operational performance, as opposed to compliance, then to what extent do you want us to report on what we already know versus identifying vulnerabilities?

Marsh Carter: The board wants to see risk management focused on performance, not just compliance. With compliance, it is too easy to fall back on checklists and then get hurt by a real risk. We need both views, but retrospective reporting should be providing insight to prevent future problems and should not distract us from the next risk coming at us. This also pushes us past compliance-limited views of the amount of risk the board is willing to take, to views based on real operations and how that interacts with the real business environment.

Karen Osar: Performance must be primary. If we don't focus on performance, we go out of business and compliance is just a closing exercise. Also, if performance is the focus, this automatically answers a number of secondary questions. For example, some compliance people wring their hands over the 'reporting threshold'—how bad something has to be to report it. If the focus is on performance, then two points are clear. First, managers must be addressing 'little things' because it is the little things that snowball into big things. Second, managers must address the little things because fixing them saves time and cost. Hiding or ignoring them just lets the problem fester and wastes resources.

Humphrey Polanen: There is always a concern that the compliance focus will take more effort and time than the performance focus. As a public company, we need to focus on performance. We've taken several actions to keep the focus on performance.

What do you suggest to close the accountability/ownership gap? Significant progress has been made, but the level of accountability and ownership of the operational-risk processes, the quality of the control environment, and so on is still sub-optimum.

Mark Olson: I want assurance that all risk exposures are first of all recognized, and secondly, managed. I want to be sure that managers of operating divisions understand the importance of managing operational risk and participate actively in the process.

How do you suggest improving risk oversight in view of the complexity of operations and activities? Key processes and activities in major financial institutions are global and complex. They cross multiple business units, locations and channels. This alone would be a challenge, but is compounded by managing by line of business. This precludes an end-to-end focus and ownership of key processes. Without this, our vulnerability to large losses will remain, or even increase.

Marsh Carter: At State Street, getting to a process view was essential to our transformation of what we sold. It had to be done to generate revenue and serve customers. We could then use it for risk management as well. Assigning a senior executive with clear accountability for an end-to-end process is a start.

Ron Dietz: Process understanding is fundamental to risk management. Really, managing risk to operations is about understanding changes in the environment and changes in business process. Without deeply understanding the process, I can't understand the potential for harmful changes to occur, I can't pin-point the root causes and I can't fix it. The robo-signing problem is one example of the need to understand process.

Rick Sergel: In the electric utility business, failure to have an end-to-end view can become a major problem quickly if it cascades through the system. All utilities must share in providing the needed visibility.

How do you recommend improving the linkage between operational risk management and strategic/business planning? We could do much better in terms of understanding, analyzing and incorporating the financial and reputational impacts of operational risk into our strategic and business planning. This includes assessing operational risk on a business-by-business and product-by-product basis. This will become more important as regulation is added to over time.

Ron Dietz: If risk management and business planning are connected at the outset, linkage should occur more easily. If you need to change a process for a business reason to accommodate a new product, the risk aspect will be built in. As another example, the fusion of business planning and risk management is important in M&A. We've grown with the help of key acquisitions and learned the importance of continuously improving our operational risk management processes to enhance performance of the acquisition.

How do we create a performance-oriented view of risk management when we're too busy doing compliance? The burdens of increasing regulation and reporting requirements will be significant. This leaves little time for real risk management, such as improving frameworks or understanding the linkages between credit, market and operational risks. Time is at a premium.

Mark Olson: Yes, one obvious link is the tendency in both to under-recognize and therefore under-manage risk exposures in isolated functions. For example, in a bank with a significant branch system, a major Bank Secrecy Act/Anti-Money Laundering risk can occur at a small or isolated branch that can threaten the reputational risk of an entire organization. On the credit side, a poorly managed and controlled lending area, even when small, can become a major risk if exposure limits are exceeded or if fraud occurs.

Karen Osar: Part of the solution is simply having different teams focused on compliance, risk and performance. We don't have the same team delivering products and doing financial compliance reporting. That would defocus from performance. In the same way, risk people need to be primarily operations-focused, not primarily compliance-focused.

How do we better engage with the board to address risks due to the institution's form of governance? There is a far greater focus on governance, a part of operational risk, from regulators and other stakeholders.

Karen Osar: In one of the non-bank boards that I serve on, we have risk management reporting to the nominating and governance committee of the board of directors. This both helps cement the linkage to governance and a focus on performance.

Rick Sergel: A key concern in governance is when decision-makers' perspectives are too narrow—they don't have all the necessary information and, worse, don't realize they need to broaden their view. This is an area where the board needs to be involved to ensure that its oversight process is actually working and being passed down through the organization. It is not a single conversation—there must be an ongoing dialogue.

What do you recommend we do to improve alignment between business language and regulatory language? The Basel categories are difficult to work with because they aren't in terminology familiar to the business and are not reflective of how processes actually operate. This makes it difficult for me to engage the rest of the organization and get traction from business leaders.

The result is that business leaders tend to treat operational risk activities as a compliance process rather than a daily management activity.

Ron Dietz: Our organization faced the same problem. The categories just didn't fit our operations and didn't seem clear and consistent with each other. We finally came to the conclusion that we needed to use categories that made sense for the actual risks we faced to our daily operations. That has helped us align risk management with the rest of management. We map back when we need to.

What skill capability do you want to see in the operational risk management team? Today, operational risk managers tend to be risk management generalists rather than subject matter specialists (e.g. not IT, procurement, financial crime specialists—unlike their credit risk peers). As a result, their credibility is questioned by business leaders. The result is that operational risk managers revert to managing a process rather than risk management.

Karen Osar: I believe training is critical to success in understanding current and emerging risks across the organization. Just as we train employees to understand ethical behavior, we must train employees to identify risk. This is key to understanding risks we don't know about and emerging risks. It is critical to encourage employees always to ask, 'What could go wrong?', and then to report a perceived risk. Again, training should emphasize that there is no punishment for pointing out risks. To the contrary, identifying and reporting risks is highly valued behavior. While we always have security, ethical, compliance and related guidelines to govern both behavior and process management, employee awareness is also a powerful tool in risk management.

How do we talk to our regulators about expectations? There is, I believe, ambiguity within our regulators as to what 'good' looks like. They tend to focus more on risk measurement and less on risk management (until things go wrong).

Ron Dietz: Conversation. As board members, we go to conferences just like you do and talk with regulators and other board members. Sometimes different agencies will be asking for different information because they are responding to different missions and regulations themselves. In any event, the attitude needs to be: 'You don't need to struggle through this alone, let's talk it through together.'

Mark Olson: Meeting regulatory expectations is always a challenge, but it is a particularly difficult challenge with operational risk, as the regulatory guidance is less specific than in other compliance areas. My suggestion is to avoid the trap of trying to get by with meeting just the minimum regulatory expectations. A well-thought-through and carefully executed approach should meet regulatory expectations. Obviously, this presumes that the bank is fully aware, and within the parameters, of all the regulatory guidance.

What can we do together to make the board's interest in operational risk more transparent to the organization in order to motivate action and build risk awareness into the company culture? I know that the board is engaged on the topic. The difficulty is that the rest of the organization doesn't see your level of involvement and the priority you place on getting this right.

Humphrey Polanen: We invite a number of managers to speak to the board meetings, rather than spending time creating packages. We want to hear directly what is happening. Getting more people involved makes it clearer.

Rick Sergel: Get many different people at different levels and with different backgrounds all sharing with the board. Encourage a flow of managers and ideas. Don't rely on mechanical reporting. Assume members want to hear from you and want all information. This gets more leaders engaged on the subject.

What would you like to see in better reporting to the board? Also, what convenient system can we put in place to ensure that reports are reviewed, questions are asked and answered in a timely way, and actions plans are tracked to closure?

Mark Olson: When risks were identified or problems occurred, I want them to be aggressively addressed and promptly reported to the board. This can be accomplished through periodic reports that include a subjective evaluation of the potential risk, the probability of the risk occurring and a description of how the risk issue is being addressed.

Karen Osar: Because of my emphasis on training and capability, I also want to see status on what both operational risk and human resources are doing to train the risk management function and the organization as a whole. Everyone has a role in risk.

Humphrey Polanen: Cutting through the clutter of data is important. I keep working on the dashboard to have clarity on KPIs and get early warnings from directly related KRIs. The need is for analytics to get early warning and take action to make a difference. Data that gets to the risk management steering committee or the board 30 to 60 days after the fact is not an early warning. So data is the biggest problem to better risk management on an operational level. This can be addressed through improved core systems (where asset values are) and then in the risk management systems and dashboards.

Rick Sergel: Let's see the scenarios. The scenarios should tell a full story of how risks develop and cascade through a system to impact real operations.

4.3. Conclusion: Your Opportunity to Make a Difference

This book has endeavored to present a practical path to a more systematic, business-performance-focused operational risk management. This is a vision that comes from operational risk managers around the world who tell me they want to:

- demonstrate business value, not just compliance cost, to their board and executive management

- engage the business

- have a 'seat at the table': recognition for adding value and participation in key business initiatives such as acquisitions and new products

- solve, not just raise, problems for business leaders

- meet the requirements of regulators with a program that is proactive and includes the latest guidance

- save time and cost

- invest wisely in building the right risk management skills

- reduce operational-risk capital through real risk reduction.

As we've seen through the panel, it is not only operational risk leaders who are seeking improved maturity that is more performance-focused, but also the board members.

Improved, more performance-focused operational risk is achievable. Risk management leaders of many types have successfully used these approaches for decades. Improvement can also come by recovering what was done in the past in financial institutions. These improvements don't need to come with a huge price tag. First, many approaches are designed to improve efficiency and effectiveness in the risk management process. Second, they all contribute to improved business performance. In public presentations, I share with audiences one of my personal metrics—to achieve in six weeks what would have taken six months. This can also become within your reach.

You can draw on the experience of thousands of risk professionals with whom the author, contributors, panellists and reviewers have worked over the years. You can make a difference in your institution.

To summarize, an operational-risk process cycle was introduced for improving the maturity and quality of outcomes. The cycle is time-sensitive as a whole and at each of its steps. Time matters—the speed of change in environment, capability, unfolding situations, time to prepare, to build capability, to reposition, and speed of reaction and recovery.

Risk to operations management cycle

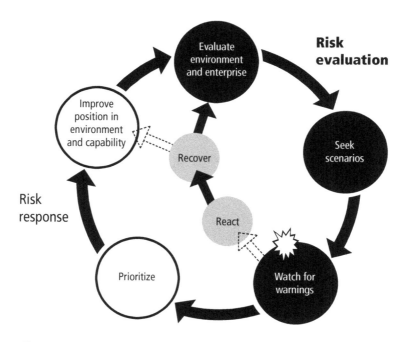

Figure 43

Evaluating risk

- **Take a systems view of risk**—the environment and enterprise capabilities. **Scenarios are your central tool for understanding situations in time**.

- Take a prospective, not retrospective, view of risk evaluation.

- Understand the environment better than competitors. This is a requirement in strategy and operations. It's also a requirement in managing risk to your strategy and operations.

- Understand the business. A deep understanding of how it works is essential to finding and fixing risks before they cause damage, and for using your capabilities to take advantage of opportunities in a changing environment.

- Look for change. Change brings threats and opportunity.

- Find the person who already knows—few risks are truly new in the world.

- Identify the right performance measures and data.

- Select the right tool (approaches, methods, techniques) for the job. Maturing organizations need more efficient tools to be effective more easily.

- **Relentlessly ask, 'What if?', 'When?' and 'How long?'** Bring together the understanding of the environment and how the business works through robust scenarios to understand how to seize opportunities and guard against loss.

- Be honest. Rigorously check for bias. Markets, shareholders, competitors, customers and regulators will find them if you don't. Understand causes and types of bias and root them out before they hurt the business and you look foolish.

- Be vigilant. Watch for warning signs in the environment, capability weakness and outcomes. Minimize lag time and static to create meaningful early warning indicators.

- Drive risk evaluation to improve business performance. Focusing on real performance should also cover the more narrow compliance exercise.

Responding to risk

- In responding to risk, understand your options and the value of keeping them open. Scrutinize decisions that would foreclose your options to prevent or react to risk.

- Time matters—understand the implications at each step of the cycle.

- Take advantage of the wide range of proven approaches to reduce risk from disciplines such as business process improvement/reengineering, quality control, software application development, business continuity, crisis management, strategic planning and financial management.

- Select from the range of tools/techniques to help clarify risk response priorities for action.

- Tools are ways to make capability improvement easier. Capability improvements are levers (in both the risk management and competitive strategy sense) for improvements in outcomes. Create levers!

- Make the distinction between response to risks that are environment related (usually external and non-process driven), and those that are process-related.

- Make a distinction between strengthening capabilities in oversight, management, controls and the business product process (analyze, develop, market, sell, deliver, support).

- Partner with other teams in the institution with objectives to improve process, grow profitable revenue and/or protect from risk.

- Efficient and effective command and control capabilities are crucial to being able to react fast enough to minimize loss and/or take advantage of opportunity.

- Once a problem occurs, the focus is on slowing or stopping the cascade of events to reduce the impact and consequences. Success in reducing is dependent on underlying business process capability, preparedness, controls and early warning situational awareness.

- Rapid recovery largely depends on quickly finding the root cause of the change, understanding environment and/or process, and advance preparations for recovery.

- Improvements over the longer term are the only true way to risk reduction. Heroic, shorter-term fixes are needed to stay in business, but efficient risk response depends on improvements in capabilities and positioning within or reshaping the environment.

- Understanding controls in basic terms makes it easier to make controls more effective in finding and fixing problems and more efficient to implement, maintain and test.

- Product management discipline can help engage the institution to reduce a range of risks, such as fraud, while improving business outcomes.

- IT risk grows as institutions become more dependent on technology. Established tools can help you map dependencies, and avoid product and process problems.

- Your opportunity as an operational risk leader is to harness the range of proven tools, engage the expertise with these tools in your institution and then to: 1) use risk management insight to apply this capability to the top priorities for risk reduction and 2) lead the team to solutions that are faster, better and cheaper than would have occurred otherwise. This creates shareholder value.

Oversight and governance of risk

- Governance is about getting the right information to the right people at the right time to make the right (or at least better) decisions.

- Governance, strictly speaking, is about board-of-directors' oversight of management. Governance can also be formally delegated to bodies of managers, especially for oversight of projects that cross silos within the institution.

- Governance is distinct from the risk management cycle and the institution's core business-product process cycle. Problems in each of these cycles must be understood and fixed to have healthy risk management that drives performance and compliance with laws, regulations and contracts.

- More risk-aware decisions that better balance risk and return must be the key process objective. These are supported with a common view of risk, standard risk-analysis templates and risk budgets.

- Risk culture is crucial; it can tear down or support risk management success. One key measure is the attitude toward finding and fixing fast. Culture that discourages finding and reporting problems (regardless of formal policy) is in danger.

- Operational risk management is embedded into enterprise-wide risk management and business management by connecting the dots with related organizational bodies, processes and communication flows. Remember, this is not only more effective, it is also more efficient. Making risk-aware decisions on the front-lines of management and fixing weaknesses in processes is better than just layering on more controls and audit.

- Risk governance and risk management are evaluated with specific tools. An example is the governance health check that evaluates whether governance is informed, transparent, accountable and agile. All evaluations must focus on finding and fixing true root cause.

Touchstones

Overall

Risk management is about *managing risk to business performance* against *specific outcomes or objectives*.

Changing situations may bring gain or loss.

Risk management is not a paperwork exercise for compliance. Compliance will always leave gaps and exposures to real business risk that can harm customers, partners and shareholders. Look at the litter of companies who were compliant and still suffered loss.

Risk management should *improve agility*, making it safer to move in a changing environment.

Risk evaluation

Root cause is the key to finding and fixing risks to performance—especially to finding problems early and fixing fast.

A *systems view* of risk is needed to understand the *dependencies* of products on processes, people and technology.

An event is not isolated. Potential and realized risks are *chains* of events that cascade in *time*, triggered by causes in dependencies or other related events.

Thus, risks must be analyzed in *robust scenarios* that consider environments, systems and cascades to understand how situations might be prevented and, when they arise, contained.

Scenarios are therefore the central feature of risk evaluation.

Little is truly unexpected in the world. After each situation arises, people often emerge who have already tried to call attention to the problem.

A key role of the operational risk manager in conducting scenario-analysis workshops is simply to *ensure that the right people are in the room* to bring their insights to the discussion of how products and processes work in systems—the dependencies, the timing, the gaps and what is already broken or likely to break under stress.

You must *push to see enough* to understand potential problems and opportunities in a changing environment.

Understand the business *value of your options*: the value of knowing now, rather than later; the value of acting now, rather than later—having *more time to act*; the value of having several possible responses, rather than being forced into one.

Risk response

Always have a plan B. Use this not only to prevent and prepare, but also to test the quality of your risk evaluation.

Base responses on *root-cause data* which can provide early warnings and point to what to fix, not proximate-cause data.

View *risk-status data in the context of cascading events in time* created earlier in scenario analysis. This gives meaning to data ('What could happen next?') and provides insight for action. This is *situational awareness*. Look for changes and *patterns* that create the need to act.

Use plan B to guide you under pressure to take the *right action*, instead of making the situation worse. Consider the cost/benefit of the range of options.

Risk oversight

More *risk–return aware decisions* are the path to reducing risk to performance.

Ensure board-level (especially independent member) engagement in operational risk.

The board *risk committee needs to have skill* in risk management and a wide range of risk types.

The chief risk officer must have clear authority and 'voice' to the board.

Match the level of assurance to the nature of each risk. 'Reasonable assurance' used for risk to financial statement preparation (and audit committees) is not sufficient for managing risk to a business initiative or risk to human safety.

Continually *improve maturity* of risk management *capability*.

Stress a culture of *find early, fix fast*, with a mandate for open communications (full disclosure, no defensiveness). Become *time-sensitive*.

Deeply build risk awareness and risk response into the organization. Everyone has a role in preventing and responding.

Be *humble*. Realize limitations. Understand bias. Seek people, training and past lessons to *overcome blind spots*.

Demand an *end-to-end view* of risk by business activity/product/process— cross the silos.

Don't forget

As you complete this book, my hope is that you have clear thoughts on how you can tailor this vision to your institution, select the tools to help you take your next steps, and feel energized to seek a new level of educational and action-oriented conversation with your executive management and board of directors.

Please remember:

- we all manage risk; it's part of life
- risk management is simple
- life and business are complex

- use risk management approaches to make business simpler as one way to reduce risk

- use risk management to provide clarity and logic, not emotion and bias

- use the right tools to make the job easier.

For the last word, we'll turn to Rick Sergel and the challenge he issued to a conference of operational risk managers:

> "These are difficult times, these are changing times. What happens in financial services today will have lasting implications. Careers will be made and broken. I encourage you to step up to this opportunity and make a difference in your institution and our financial system."

Index

Lightning Source UK Ltd.
Milton Keynes UK
UKHW02f1653120418
320931UK00003B/288/P